TABLE OF CONTENTS

The Lease or Buy Decision --

Factors that Determine the Financial Requirement of

Business Organizations

CHAPTER ONE

INTRODUCTION

THE NATURE AND SCOPE OF BUSINESS FINANCE

The subject, Finance, was originally a part of Economies. The role of the T finance manager were keeping accurate financial records, preparing reports, managing the firms cash position, providing means of paying bills, procuring additional funds externally (both long and short term). Recent development in finance led to the expansion of financial functions.

in firm and the inclusion of functions like investment of funds in assets and

obtaining best mix of financing and the overall valuation of the firm. 1920's saw the emergence of new technologies, new industries, new investment opportunities. All these led to the need for more external

procurement of funds to finance firms and to solve liquidity problems. The Great Depression of the 1930's led business managers to address the problems in areas of sound capital structure (debt plus net worth), liquidity (cash flows), bankruptcy, reorganization, restructuring and government regulation of the securities market. The emphasis was to protect the external lender.

Despite these measures, various abuses came to light during the period the companies went bankrupt and collapsed. This again led to the call for greater financial disclosures in areas like lease, depreciation, sources and application of funds, and the emergence of financial analysis as a discipline in finance.

Between 1940 and 1950 the development of cash flow, planning and control of cash were introduced into finance, but from the point of view of the external analyst. Capital budgeting became important by the middle of 1950's. The financial management of corporate asset and optimal allocation of financial resources were recognized.

The major emphasis was how financial decisions affect the value of the irm in asset, management. A quantitative measure was introduced in the col valuation of firms to allay the fears of collapse of companies by investors and creditors. For example, linear programming models to aid managers to maximize value of firm; effects of capital structure; dividend policy on the value the firms were areas of interest.

Today, as in the 1930's, the problems of cash flows, capital structure and solvency, working capital management and cash budgeting are receiving fresh pectus. It also includes financial planning and forecasting in the face of world ide inflation and uncertain future events. Equally of interest are treatment of cost of capital, sources and types of both short- and long-term finances. This overed both the money and capital markets and the characteristics of the different types of securities.

THE MEANING OF FINANCE The term finance can acquire different meanings at any given point in me depending on the context of use. As a subject, it is very broad; thus asking it almost impossible to have one straight "off the mill" definition that covers the whole subject matter. Perhaps that explains why even the dictionary explanation of the word finance is not

specific for instance, the OXFORD ADVANCED LEARNERS'
DICTIONARY OF CURRENT ENGLISH describes finance as
"the science of or the management of money or simply
money". From this description, three distinct definitions of
finance can be seen viz:

Finance defined simply as money.

Finance defined as the management of money. Finance
defined as a scientific study of money.

A fourth possible definition is to see finance as the provision of
money or

monetary support to an individual or enterprise. The first sense
in which finance simply means money is very common
especially to the layman. It is in this sense that we often say
that an organization is either in good or bad finances...
meaning that the organization has adequate funds (money) or
that it lacks money. This concept of finance is. however
narrow.

A broader concept of finance, which is perhaps more
technical, is that which views finance as the management of
money. The management of money transcends all levels of
human activity from the individual through the corporate
bodies to the government. At the individual level, the financial
problem is how to maximize his well-being using the resources
available to him Finance for the individual therefore deals with
how the individual shares his income between consumption
and investment, how he raises money to provide for additional
consumption or saving and how he makes his choice among
several investment opportunities. At the corporate level, the
objective is usually to maximize the shareholders wealth.
Finance in this respect will therefore deal with the various
sources and costs of funds and their alternative uses for the
purpose of achieving the corporate goal. Governments at

various levels also face the problems of raising money and effectively allocating same to meet the stated objectives. It can be seen that finance, viewed as the management of money permeates all aspects of our daily life. Little wonder therefore that finance has gradually evolved as a discipline/course of study.

Finance as a discipline has been variously described by many authors. For instance, a Harvard Economist - John Kenneth Galbraith thinks of finance as the study of money... whence it came and where it went. A more comprehensive description of finance is given by Lawrence D. Schall and Charles W. Harley:

According to them, finance is "a body of facts, principles, and theories dealing with the raising and using of money by individuals, businesses and governments". It also includes the study of financial institutions and markets and the activities of governments especially those that are relevant to the financial decisions of firms and individuals. This is because the flow of funds from the areas of surplus (surplus economic units) to the areas of need (deficit economic units) is done through these institutions within the confines of accepted rules and regulations. Thus far we have seen that finance as a discipline is broad based. It then follows that for effective coverage and proper understanding of the subject, it is necessary to divide it into different sub-themes such as Personal Finance, International Finance, Financial Institutions, Public Finance, Business Finance, etc. We are concerned with the study of the problem of raising and allocating financial resources for effective business operations. Nevertheless, we shall draw upon the other areas of finance those facts that are necessary for the proper understanding of our subject.

On the other hand, the meaning of finance can be interpreted to mean the provision of money. It is in this wise that we can say that STARBEST NIG. LTD will finance the 2005 NUGA

GAMES suggesting that the above-named company will provide the money for the games.

Naturally, many students usually seek in vain for a standard definition of the term Finance as a starting point for launching into the study of the study. The reason authors customarily shy away from giving a definition is presumably that the subject has mainly utilitarian origins covering a broad spectrum of activities which were hardly fixed throughout its formative years, relating to money or management of money. In the circumstance of the evolving content and the changing emphasis of finance, a standard definition would be far too inadequate to capture its full scope and relevance. Rather, a broad descriptive and explanatory definition of the nature and scope of finance will be offered and, in the course, therefore, hopefully providing some theoretical foundation for the discussions and analyses which are undertaken within this text.

Although, it is usually mentioned that finance is the live wire of any organization, in a restricted sense, Finance means money affairs, money matters, and any form of money or near money which include cash, debt certificates, share certificates debt, bank and all forms of assets which are capable of being expressed in monetary terms available to organizations or individuals for effective and efficient business and financial transactions. In certain usage, however, not only are liquid funds subsumed in the term Finance but also all forms of assets which are capable of being converted into cash within relatively short period. This usage recognizes that tangible (non-cash) assets are merely alternative forms in which individuals or entities may choose to hold their wealth. Thus in a broader sense, Finance may be said to incorporate not only money fund but also any form of asset which has a money denominator and which is capable of being transformed at some time or other at least in the intermediate term into cash.

In the study of Business Finance, one is confronted with this apparent fluidity in usage because of the role of money not only as a medium for procuring other forms of value but also as a common denominator for expressing all values. This highly utilitarian character of money, of finance, makes it an important resource and consequently a subject that is extremely interesting but complex to study.

THE MEANING OF BUSINESS A Business is a commercial endeavour which identifies a need or a gap

and of providing goods or services designed to satisfy such need with a view to profiting, earning returns, rewards and benefits. Business is creative economic activity having a wide-ranging social impact. In view of Peter Drucker (1968 52) "a business enterprise is an organ of society. There is only one valid definition of business purpose to create a customer...

The specific the 00000000above conception of business is sufficiently general as to encompass business practices of the different socio-economic systems. characteristics of business enterprise would however differ to some extent depending on the ideological setting in which it operates, that is, whether it be a capitalist or a socialist environment. Whilst in a capitalist situation, profit. Le the excess of revenue over cost, would be a principal objective or motivation for undertaking a business activity, profit thus defined may be totally absent or if at all relevant, less crucial in a socialist situation. In the context of this book the capitalist environment is assumed where individual actions are customarily motivated primarily by self-interest, and any benefits, to society as a whole. resulting from such action occur mainly because of the "invisible hand" theory enunciated by Adam Smith.

It is not always agreed that profit should be defined as the excess of revenue over cost. An alternative concept of profit is offered in centrally planted economies. This concept sees profit basically as the quantity or amount by which actual output exceeds that target, determined invariably on the basis of some motion of standard. This concept of profit which is of the nature of a "favourable variance" is not applicable the analysis undertaken in this text since it fails to throw light on the extent of growth in total wealth as a result of the entrepreneurial or managerial efforts,

The concept of business that is assumed applicable in free enterprise capitalist economics has the orthodox profit motive although there seems to be no perfect agreement about whether such profit motive is fundamental to business or merely a constraint on it, nor on the issue concerning whether business ordinarily seek to maximize profits or merely endeavour, as a minimum, to cover the risks of economic activity. The different standpoints taken on these issues may be exemplified. For instance, the assumption in mere-economic theory basically not only implies the fundamental importance of profit but in fact upholds the view that business enterprise do seek to maxima profits

Advancing a contrary view however Peter Drucker (1968: 51-2) states that it is the first duty of a business is to create a customer. The guiding principle of business activities, in other words, is not the maximization of profits but to give value to some customer.

"This does not mean that profit and profitability are unimportant t does mean that profit is not the purpose of business but a limiting factor on it Profit is not the explanation, cause or rationale of business behaviour and business decisions but the text of their validity, the problem of any business is not the maximization of profit but the achievement of sufficient profit to cover the risks of economic activity and thus to avoid loss In a similar vein. Cryert and March (1963 115-127) while admitting the importance of profit to business enterprise, draw attention to several practical difficulties which impede the attainment of maximum profits in typical business situations. These include the absence of, or excessive cost of, adequate information relevant for a perfect rational decision, the difficulty of search for all viable alternatives, the absence of perfect goal congruence among all management intense and then between management as a group and the shareholder group, etc. Cyert and March argue that as a result of these problems management decisions and actions could not be said to result from a perfect agreement on what is the best interest of the firm, but often reflect at best a distillation of divergent views and goals which inherently fall short of the requirement to achieve the best results.

In particular, attention has in recent times been drawn to the potential conflict between the interest of management which is the dominant class and those of the shareholders which exercise only remote control over company polices, and the effect which this situation may have for the ability of the firm to pursue or achieve the profit objective. It is speculated that management as a group may be more interested in safety, stability, and survival which guarantee their careers and positions than say, high profits with the attendant high risk; whereas the shareholders may on the other hand be more interested in high income than stability, since they have a greater ability to hedge against the attendant risk through portfolio diversification. Since management has the dominant influence on company performance, however, it may be inferred that companies, even if they could attain maximum profits, probably do not Management's quest for stability in preference for high income, would appear to impose on the firm the objective to make just enough profits to enable a "Satisfactory" dividend to be paid to the shareholders, while leaving a reasonable amount to maintain the capital position in the face of technological changes and inflation and to pursue a certain rate of growth.

In spite of the apparent divergence in views concerning the relevance of profit, the basic position taken in financial management literature is that profit is a principal impetus to business entrepreneurship. This seems to confirm the observed behaviour of business entrepreneurs, the complexity introduced by the dichotomy between management and ownership notwithstanding. There is also general acceptance that profit does serve to assure survival, is an indicator of success, and yields the wherewithal for meeting the proprietary and social responsibility commitments of the firm and for pursuing growth. It is of course recognized that businesses do have other objectives apart from profit, c.g. market share, prestige of owner or management, etc. but these competing goals could not be pursued for long by a company that does not earn at least a satisfactory level of profit.

The profit motive is important again because it distinguishes a business enterprise from a social service institution. The latter may or may not pursue any profit. The local environment readily presents numerous examples of business enterprise. They are invariably privately owned, although in mixed economies some business firms have been established by government. These operate especially in the strategic sectors of mining e.g. petroleum, iron and steel, air transportation and communication. The essential character of

business in capitalist and mixed economies is that they are owned and controlled by those who subscribe the equity capital and who expect to earn a return there from. Business firms invariably occur in three types of organizational forms,

namely sole proprietorship, partnership and incorporated joint stock companies. The latter category includes registered limited liability companies as well as statutory companies established by government. Each of these organizational forms has its distinct legal and control implications: Only incorporated concerns enjoy a legal personality status. Each capitalist economy features a considerable number of each of the three organization forms. A distinguishing factor among the different organizational forms is the

size of operations which is itself a function of the amount of the equity investment. By far the largest operations and investment belong to the incorporated concerns. Partnership firms follow in size. The sole proprietorship firms are often the smallest. The predominance of the incorporated concerns is the result of the enormous facility with which it is ordinarily and legally endowed to mobilize funds. In terms of the total volume of wealth controlled, and the significance and impact of their activities on the total economy, the incorporated company is undoubtedly the most important organizational form Most non-incorporated businesses usually aspire to attain the limited liability status. Because of the overriding importance of this organizational form, discussions in business and financial management usually assume it. A characteristic feature of the limited liability company is the separation in law and often also in practice between the ownership and management. The separation conforms to the basic conception of a limited liability company as a joint stock company which may be owned by a large number of individuals, who could not all, from a practical standpoint, find it feasible or convenient to become actively involved in the day to day management of the business. The legal distinction (separation) between ownership and management has far- reaching practical significance.

As already pointed out, it does have implications for the validity of the theoretical supposition concerning the fundamental objective of business, that is, whether businesses do actually seek to maximize or even optimize profit or owner's wealth. In view of this and other factors already considered, it would seem that the position taken by Cyert and March and also by Peter Drucker. that businesses only seek to earn a satisfactory level of profit, is a more realistic representation of the objective of business than the classical microeconomic theory..

Business finance, therefore, can be said to be money affairs and money matters available to commercially oriented enterprise for the purpose of providing goods or services to satisfy identified need or gap for economic benefits.

THE PURPOSE OF A BUSINESS

To know what a business is we have to start with its purpose. Its purpose must lie outside the business itself. In fact, it must lie in society, since business enterprise is an organ of society. There is only one valid definition of

business purpose: TO CREATE A CUSTOMER.

It is the customer who determines what a business is. It is the customer alone whose willingness to pay for a good or for a service converts economic resources into wealth, things into goods. What the business thinks it produces is not of first importance- especially not to the future of the business and to its

success.

The typical engineering definition of quality is something that is hard to do, is complicated, and costs a lot of money! But that isn't quality; it's incompetence.

What the customer thinks he or she is buying, what he or she considers value, is decisive it determines what a business is, what it produces, and - whether it will prosper. And what the customer buys and considers value is never a product. It is always utility. That is, what a product or service does for

him or her.

Customers are foundation of a business and keep it in existence. They alone give employment. To supply the wants and needs of a customer, society entrusts wealth producing resources to the business enterprise. In furtherance of the purpose of a business, in formulating policy and

developing strategies and tactics, an organization must have a purpose(s) which.

it hopes to achieve with the policies and strategies. These purposes, could be

defined as its MISSION, GOALS and OBJECTIVES.

A corporate MISSION is the broad purpose which the society within which the organization is operating expects it to serve. It is the linkage between the organization and its external environment. Statement of corporate missions are to be found in the Memoranda of Association of organizations. Corporate missions are thus used to legitimize specific programmes. For instance, "To Provide Service to Society and aid economic development" or "keeping Country Moving (Michelin) are both statements of missions as they are broad, vague and quite often value-laden statements of purposes that lack any specificity. Thus a mission defines the broad objective, the unique aim that sets the organization apart from others of its type. Hence the Bank says:

"Our mission is to offer prompt and efficient services of the most excellent quality and to provide imaginative financial products to be marketed through our extensive branch network throughout world."

This is what ACB stands for and what gives it its strategic direction. On the other hand John Holt Limited has a more detailed view of its corporate mission.

"The mission of John Holt Limited is to engage in manufacturing, industrial, commercial, financial and other related business that provide goods and services that best meet the nee ds of the world.

CHAPTER TWO

STATEGIC FINANCIAL OBJECTIVES OF BUSINESS ORGANISATION

WHAT IS A STRATEGY?

F Nor a policy to be meaningful, for financial objectives to be successfully achieved, there must be some operational strategy that will translate the into courses of action. Strategies are means of operationalising a policy and for achieving some predetermined objectives.

According to Anao (1979) "strategies are schemes, methods, manoeuvres

which management hopes to deploy in order to move the organization from its

present position to arrive at its target goal by the end of a specified period.

take place in the environment".

Thomas (1977) on the other hand sees strategy as "the determination of

recognizing that during the intervening period a host of changes are going to The general Electric Company sees strategy as "a statement of what resources are going to be used to take advantage of which opportunities, to minimize which threats and to produce a desired result".

basic long range goals and objectives and the adoption of courses of action with the allocation of the necessary resources

Glueck (1984) defines strategy as "a unified, comprehensive and integrated plant relating the strategic advantages of the firm to the challenges of the environment. It is designed to ensure that the basic objectives of the enterprise are achieved".

For Stainer and Miner (1977) strategy is "the forging of company

missions, setting of objectives for the organization in the light of external and

internal forces, formulating policies and strategies to achieve objectives and

assuring their proper implementation so that the basic purpose and objective of

the organisation will be achieved".

Christensen, Andres and Bower (1978) argue that corporate strategy pattern of decisions in a company that:

is a

(a) Shapes and reveals its objectives, purposes and goals; (b) (c) Produces the principal policies and plans for achieving these goals; Defines the kind of business and the kind of economic and human organization it intends to be.

Equally, Schellenberger and Boseman (1978) see strategy as hierarchical system of basic objectives, fulfilling objectives and policies as well a as establishing the plans and allocating the resources to achieve the objectives. Both authors see the hierarchy as basically three tiers: the first consisting of basic objectives, the second containing the fulfilment of objectives, and the third as being made up of policies.

According to Benjamin (2001) strategy is defined as "a course including the specification of the resources required, to achieve a specific objective. It is the development of resources to achieve specific objective. The major aims of

strategy include: To determine the direction the organisation will move in the long-term.
(1)

16
To determine the scope of the organisation's activities, eg, it's product market range

To match the activities of the organization with its resource capacity

(iv) To plan the allocation of corporate resources

To direct the activities of the organization towards achieving the values expectations and goals of people or coalition, affected by the organisation's results

To maximize the organisation's strengths

(vi)

(vii)

To reduce the organisation's weaknesses (vin) To exploit as far as possible the opportunities open to the organization To monitor and control activities

(ix)

In concluding these various definitions in the literature. Newman and Logan (1976) say strategy is concerned with where an organization should be headed in the future. It concentrates on the major moves to be taken by the particular company at the present stage in her development. In essence, a strategy is a chosen course of action for pursuing an objective. For a business organization "strategic decisions are primarily concerned with external rather than internal problems of the firms and specifically with the selection of the product mix which the firm will produce and the markets to which it will sell", (Ansoff, 1984). In other words, a business firm which chooses to pursue the profit objective will have to contend with the strategies for achieving it through what products it should produce and sell (product mix) and where it intends to sell them (markets) in the light of the intentions of other competing firms

PRODUCT MISSION PRESENT

PRESENT

FUTURES

Expansion (Market Penetration)

Product

FUTURE

Market Development

development Diversification

A company or organization trying to grow profitably must decide on its strategic options as in figure 1. It can either choose to expand its present market through penetration or develop new markets for the future if the present ones are saturated by competition. On the other hand, it can choose the strategic opinion of developing new products for the future in its present markets to upstage the competition or diversify into new areas entirely ot stabilize income. But as Ansoff argues, as an organization grows and expands

17
towards deintensification it is expected that its strategies will change in response to growth

However, whatever strategic options that an organization develops and chooses they must be strictly within the framework of pre-established policy. For as Ansoff! further argues, strategy is dirvelispadlim a generalized form and its meaning sharpened, clarified and tested by polity Indeed
"no strategy has really heem thought out through untill its implications for policy (and programmes)) have been espined! (Newman and Logan 1976). Strategy must thus be supported by policy and policy rationalized and justified by effective strategies.

FACTORS THAT SHAPE STRATEGY (a) Opportunities identified in the environment.

Organisational competence and resource capabilities.

Threats to opportunities in the environment

Social obligations and ethical values.

Organisational culture and value system innovative, complacent,, are bureaucratic. whether pioneering,

BOTE: A Policy is a guide for making demonstrative decisions. In other words, a policy i am internal administrative laws governing executive actions within the organisation.

LEVEL OF STRATEGY

Strategy can be developed at three levels:

Corporate Strategy This is concerned with the broad issues, such as which types of business

the company should be in. Strategic finance has an important role to play here. For example the decision to enter or exit from a business, whether through corporate acquisitions, organic growth, divestment or Buy-outs requires sound financial analysis.

Similarly, the decision as to the appropriate capital structure and

dividend policy form part of strategic development at the corporate

level.

2. Business or Competitive Strategy This is concerned with how strategic business units (S B Us) compete in particular markets. Business strategies are formulated which influence the allocation of resources to these units. Porter (1985) identifies five competitive forces that determine the profitability of an industry. Threat of Patas ta Barts-New entrants to the industry will increase total productive capacity and this can result in price wars and reduced profitability. The size of the threat is determined by entries barrier carented by such things as differentiation of

products, the capital requirement and economies of scale.

(b)

Competition Among Existing Companies: Intensive cavalry is the result of factors such as numerous or equally balanced competitors, slow industrial growth and a high level of feed charges in the cost structures, i.e. operational gearing. (c)

Pressure from Substitutes: While firms compete within an industry, the industry itself also competes in the sense that other industries can often deliver substitute products. For example, the oil industry offers a substitute product for the all industry. In the case of a price increase, customers may shift from one to the

other.

Bargaining Power of Suppliers: Suppliers can considerable pressure on an industry to threatening to raise prices or to cut the quality off goods and services delivered.

(e) Bargaining Power of Buyers: Buyers matte a competitive finance, exerting a downward pressure on prices, negotiating for higher quality or better service and playing off one competitor against another, all at the expense of the industry's profitability

Careful analysis of the above factors enable managers to understand better the major competitive factors which shape the industry and thereby, determine the levels of profitability a company can expect to earn. A business strategy stands little chamoe of success unless developed with a clear understanding of the firm's competitive setting. Each of the five competitive forces will vary from industry to industry and importance according to the industry in which the firm operates

3: Operating Strategy

This is concerned with row functional levels contribute to corporate and business strategies. For examples, the finance functionary formulate strategies to achieve the new dividend policy identified at the corporate strategy level. Similarly, a foreign currency exposure strategy may be developed to reduce the risk of loss through currency movements.

FINANCIAL GOALS AND THEIR ATTAINMENT

Business organization usually set for itself financial goals which include the maximization of profits - the primary goal. In this context, maximization of profits means maximization of the wealth of the company, which translates into the maximization of the wealth of the shareholders.

Significantly, maximization of profits is quite different from making of profits. For every profit maximization, there is profit making, but profit making does not necessarily accommodate profit maximization. Profit maximization generally means a situation whereby business organisation's profit earning pattern has linear relationship/curve from year to year. When the profit pattern of such organization is graphed for a number of years, the curve slops upward

19

(d) from left to right. Simply put, maximization of profits connote that profit earning history of the organization continue to be on the increase. On the other hand, making of profit is defined as the ability of business organisation to earn a revenue or income higher than the cost of operations. Under this scenario, profit earning ability may either be galloping, showing downwards or decreasing from year to year.

Considering the fact that inflation is always on the increase, compounding and increasing the prices of materials labour, overheads and other factors of production, it becomes imperative that business organizations should strive at profit maximization in order to cope with the unprecedented effect of inflation as well as enjoying the "going concern" status.

To attain these financial goals, the various sections, divisions, departments and segments in the organisation are expected to work as a team. Regular and constant flow of information for an effective communication link among the departments should be encouraged. Spirit of goal congruence should be given enabling environment. State of the art facilities and equipment

should be procured to enhance performance and qualitative goods and services. Besides, adequate and sufficient finance should be at the disposal of all departments to enable them maintain functional operations. Necessary checks and balances should be put in place to eliminate the incidence of waste, fraud, embezzlement and the like. Strict control measures should be planted in the financial system and business transactions of the company to facilitate the over all growth and development of the organization.

As a matter of deliberate policy, attractive incentives and rewards should be set aside for hardworking, honest, dedicated, devoted, diligent, resourceful and committed employees, while harsh sanctions and penalties are stamped on erring workers. Conducive working environment should be created for employees. Opportunity for training, growth and development should be made available to the workers..

Moreover, good rapport should exist between the organisation and the customers, suppliers and the society in general. Customers should have value for their money, the company's financial obligations to the suppliers should be honoured as and when due. If this is not possible, timely negotiation and dialoguing is recommended. The society/community in which the company operates should have a fair share of the organisation's goodies by way of infrastructural facilities.

Enlightenment campaign should be practiced to educate the staff that the financial well being of the corporation is to their advantage, reason being that the company will be in better financial standing to meet and discharge all their pecuniary entitlements and benefits.

Concerted efforts from all and sundry will in no small way make the attainment of the financial goals a reality.

FINANCIAL OBJECTIVES OF BUSINESS ORGANISATION

As previously mentioned, every business must have an objective or objectives as bedrock upon which short-term targets can be established. Without dearly defined objectives, it is impossible to: 20
(i) develop evaluation techniques for selecting investment opportunities.

(ii)   institute suitable performance measures which will ensure that the company is moving in the right direction.

However, there is little agreement in the literature as to what objectives of firms are, or even what they ought to be. By and large, most texts subscribe to the fact that the objective of a limited company is the MAXIMIZATION of the WEALTH of its SHAREHOLERS. Maximizing the
wealth of the shareholders in the same thing as maximizing the value of equity. Most financial models are based on the quest of wealth maximization and are at least four reason are advanced for this ground.

0 The managers are normally obliged to do so as they are ultimately paid by their shareholders and are entrusted with shareholders money. The higher the share price, the easier it is to raise new finance to further

their pursuit of alternative objectives.

(i) the share price is allowed to drop to too low a level, it may attract the

attention of city predator and result in an unwelcome take-over bid. (iv) There is also the invisible hand's argument of Adam Smith that if individuals and firms pursue the goals of wealth maximization, then they

will automatically maximize the overall economic welfare of the nation.

The financial objective of maximizing the wealth of ordinary shareholders

has to be converted into planning strategies by a company's management. This can be done in a number o ways which include: (a) A company could set targets to increase the market value of its ordinary shares by a stated amount or percentage. A public company's directors might decide to set a target of increasing the share price by 20% next year and another 20% the year after. But this wouldn't be a good idea, because share prices can be easily influenced by factors outside management control, such as a change interest rates, or even political change such as change of government.

Management should set targets for factors which they are in a better position to influence directly, such as profits (earnings) and dividend growth. An so a financial objective may be expressed as the aim of increasing profits, earnings per share and dividend per share by say 10%p a. for each of the next five years.

If there is an increase in earnings and dividends, management can hope or an increase in share price too, so that shareholders benefit from both higher evenue (dividends) and also capital gains (higher share prices).

21 develop evaluation techniques for
selecting investment opportunities.

institute suitable performance measures which will ensure that the

company is moving in the right direction. However, there is little
agreement in the literature as to what objectives of firms are, or even
what they ought to be. By and large, most texts subscribe to the fact
that the objective of a limited company is the MAXIMIZATION of
the WEALTH of its SHAREHOLERS. Maximizing the wealth of
the shareholders is the same thing as maximizing the value of equity.
Most financial models are based on the quest of wealth
maximization and are at least four reason are

advanced for this ground. The managers are normally obliged to do
so as they are ultimately paid by their shareholders and are entrusted
with shareholders money.

The higher the share price, the easier it is to raise new finance their
pursuit of alternative objectives.

to further

(i) he share price is allowed to drop to too low a level, it may attract
the attention of city predator and result in an unwelcome take-over
bid.

(1) There is also the invisible hand's argument of Adam Smith that if
individuals and firms pursue the goals of wealth maximization, then
they

will automatically maximize the overall economic welfare of the
nation.

The financial objective of maximizing the wealth of ordinary
shareholders has to be converted into planning strategies by a

company's management. This can be done in a number o ways which include: a) A company could set targets to increase the market value of its ordinary

(

shares by a stated amount or percentage. A public company's directors might decide to set a target of increasing the share price by 20% next year and another 20% the year after. But this wouldn't be a good idea, because share prices can be easily influenced by factors outside management control, such as a change interest rates, or even political change such as change of government.

(b) Management should set targets for factors which they are in a better position to influence directly, such as profits (earnings) and dividend growth. An so a financial objective may be expressed as the aim of increasing profits, earnings per share and dividend per share by say 10% pa.
for each of the next five years.

If there is an increase in earnings and dividends, management can hope for an increase in share price too, so that shareholders benefit from both higher revenue (dividends) and also capital gains (higher share prices).

21

OTHER FINANCIAL TARGETS In addition to the primary and main objectives of wealth maximization

, a

company might set some other financial targets such as: (a) A restriction on the company's level of gearing, or debt. For example, a company's management might decide that: (1) the ratio of long-term debt capital to equity capital should never exceed say, 1:1

(ii)

the cost of interest payments should never be higher that say 25% of total profits before interest and tax.

(b)

(c)

A target for profit retentions. For example, management might set a target that dividend cover (the ration of distributable profit to dividends actually distributed) should not be less than say 2.5 times.

A target for operating profitability. For example, management might set a

target for the profit/sales ratio (say, a minimum of 10%) or for a return

on capital employed (say a minimum ROCE of 20%).

These financial targets are not primary financial objectives, but they can

act as subsidiary targets or constraints which should help a company to achieve

its main financial objective without excessive risk.

However, these targets are usually measured over a year rather than over the long-term, and it is maximization of shareholder wealth in the long term that ought to be the corporate objective.

Short-term measures of return can encourage a company to pursue example by deferring

short-term objectives at the expense of long-term ones, for new capital investments, or spending only small amounts on research and

development and on training. A company may have important non-financial objectives which could

NON-FINAICIAL OBJECTIVES

limit or enhance the achievement of the main financial objectives. Examples of

non-financial objectives are as follows:

1.

The welfare of employees

Companies accept that the interests of employees should be provided for. even if this means having to accept higher pay roll and administrative costs, and lower profits. A company might therefore try to provide good wages and salaries, comfortable and safe working conditions, and good pensions. If redundancies are necessary, many companies will provide generous redundancy payments, or spending money trying to find alternative employment For redundant staff.

Satisficing

This objective is said to be followed when management aims at accomplishing less than what is possible under the circumstances.

As stewardship of firms is divorced from ownership, this goal of satisfying is likely to prevail in real life. This is obviously not a desirable objective and will certainly not lead to the maximization of the wealth of the firm. "Satisficing" if followed by management to the extreme, will be detected and hence penalized.

3.

The Welfare of Management

Managers will often take decisions to improve the quality of their own life and circumstances, even though their decisions will incur high expenditure and so reduce profits. High salaries, company cars and other perks can all be suggested as examples of managers pursuing the objective of promoting their own interests and comfort first and foremost to the detriment of what is best for the corporate entity.

4. The Welfare of Society as a Whole (Social Responsibility) Most larger companies have accepted the challenge that they have an obligation to the society in which they operate. In this connection relentless efforts are being intensified by companies to improve the standard of living of the host community. In other words, the management of companies are aware of the role that their company has to play in providing for the well-being of

society. This may reflect itself in many ways which include:

The formulation of employment policies that avoid exploitation restriction of individuals rights.

and

Investment policies that take account of the effects of corporate activity on the physical environment. Cooperation with both local and national governments in the furtherance of national economic and social policies. Provision of infrastructural facilities to the host community in particular and the society in general. Such facilities include potable water, roads, schools, hospitals, electricity, etc. similarly, employment and scholarship should be given to qualified and deserving citizens of the host community.

No doubt, the activities and operations of the companies negatively affect not only the ecology of the host community but also pollute their land, water and air thereby making them unfit for human habitation. To compensate for this destructive act, companies cannot but be socially responsible, even though it calls for reduction in profits.

5. The Provision of Goods and Services

The major objectives of some companies will include the provision of goods and services to the public at no cost. This act normally eat deep into the profit of the organization, even when such goods and services are of qualitative nature.

In a separate development, many commercial organizations make explicit reference to the need to provide qualitative, functional quantitative goods and services to their customers and the public. This forms the cornerstone of their financial objective.

23

6

Increasing the Size of Market Share increasing the size of market share means expanding the scope of goods

and services distribution. It also involves penetrating into new customers and breaking into all nooks and crannies of the urban and rural areas. Increasing market share also connotes increasing the power, influence and remuneration packages of executives.

7. Increased Profit

This is a fairly obvious objective, but one which has some vivid difficulties. The most difficult question to answer is profit over what period. Maximizing profit in the short run may not be in the best long-term interests of the firm as a whole. Maximizing profits could mean minimizing sales. In other words, there is a trade off relationship between profit and sales maximization. Increased profit could be achieved through cost control and cost reduction as well as gentle increase in selling price.

8. Survival

Survival strategy, the most pressing, exciting and fearful objective of all and one that has exercised and threatened the minds of many financial executives in recent years. Going concern is an extension of survival objective When survival is doubtful for any organization, liquidation will come on board Survival is most prevalent in organizations between their formative and maturity stage. During this period, unprecedented losses are recorded, until break-even point is reached which eventually pave way for marginal profit.

Responsibilities Towards Customers and Suppliers Responsibilities towards customers include providing a product or service of a quality that customers expect and dealing honestly and fairly with customers.

Responsibilities towards suppliers are expressed mainly in terms of trading relationships. A company size could give it considerable power as a buyer. The company should not use its power unscrupulously. Suppliers might rely on getting prompt payment, in accordance with the agreed terms of trade.

THE RELATIONSHIP BETWEEN FINANCIAL

AND NON-FINANCIAL OBJECTIVES

Non-financial objectives do not cancel out financial objectives, but they do mean that the simple theory of company finance, that the objective of a firm is to maximize the wealth of ordinary shareholders, is too simplistic and is not correct Financial objectives have to be compromised in order to satisfy non financial objectives

When company management take decisions about investment, financing dividends, etc, they must make a judgment, and balance the conflicting objectives in what seems to be the best way. So where does this leave us when

24

we approach financial management? What is the basis on which financial management theory is built? The answer is that we take as a starting point the simple view of

company finance, that a company's management should seek to maximize the wealth of its ordinary shareholders, and we try to identity how wealth- maximizing decisions should be made. In spite of the fact that this isn't realistic, it nevertheless provides useful information for management about the likely impact of the decisions they take; and the likely effect of a decision on shareholder wealth should at least influence the decision that is finally taken, even taking non-financial considerations into account. Management cannot ignore the financial consequences of their decisions.

It isn't good enough for a company to break even or make a profit. It has to

provide a return that will satisfy investors, which means that a company's profit

must reach an "accepted" minimum level. If profits and dividends aren't good enough: (a) The company will be vulnerable to a takeover bid, because its shares won't be worth as much as they would be, and a predator might be able to obtain shareholder acceptance of a takeover at a cheap price

and then set about increasing profits;

(b) The company will have trouble persuading investors to provide extra finance when it wants more funds. Investors will only put new money into a company if they think that it will earn an adequate return and

keep the value of their investment "Safe". In summary, we can say that financial management decisions must have regard to their effect on shareholder wealth, and so the basic theory of company finance is a good starting point for evaluating decisions. Non-financial matters,

however, will probably influence the decision that is finally taken, but not to the

detriment of wealth maximization.

STRATEGIC FINANCIAL OBJECTIVES FOR THE PARASTATALS

AND GOVERNMENT OWNED COMPANIES

Parastatals and government owned companies are industrial organizations, enterprises, etc having some political authority and serving the state indirectly. They are financed by government loans and grants and perhaps some "external" borrowing too from the capital markets. They do not have equity capital, hence no shareholders and there is no Stock Exchange to give a continuous valuation of the business.

Financial objectives and financial management in government are substantially at variance with what obtains in industrial and commercial companies for some fairly obvious reasons:

L.

Government departments do not necessarily operate to make profit and the objectives of a department cannot be expressed in terms of maximizing return on capital employed.

25

2.

Government goods and services are provided without the commercial pressures or competition from the market. There are no competitive reasons for controlling costs or being efficient when goods are produced or services are rendered.

3. Government departments have full time professional Civil Servants as their managers, but planning and controlling decisions are also taken by politicians.

The government gets its money for spending from taxes, other sources of income are borrowings (issuing gilt-edge etc) and the nature of its fund raising differs remarkably from that of public companies.

Financial markets regard the government as a totally "Secured borrower and so the government can usually borrow whatever it likes, provided it is

prepared to pay a suitable rate of interest. Federal government borrowing is coordinated centrally by the Treasury and Central Bank (CB). Individual department and government do not have to borrow funds themselves.

Companies rely heavily on retained profits as a sure source of funds. Government departments cannot rely on such cushion as a source because their appetite for profit making is not encouraged. In any case, some government services attract a fee to be borne by the customers, eg. Telephone, electricity, education, etc, although the price that is charged night cover the

cost in full.

The financial objectives cannot be to maximize the wealth of its owners-

the government or general public because this is not a practical concept.

Nevertheless, there will be a financial objective to contribute in a certain way to

the national economy. This objective may be varied according to the political

views of the government of the day:

(a) There may be an objective to earn sufficient profits so that the industry can provide a certain proportion (or even the entire amount) of its investment needs from its own resources, this is in line with government's objective of commercializing some parastatals; (b) A very profitable parastatal may be expected to lend surplus fund to the government.

Even so, the principal objective of a parastatal will in many cases not be a financial one at all, instead that of welfarism. The government agrees upon strategic objectives with each parastatal. These objectives may consist of a mixture of

(a)

Statutory objective which are set out in the Act which created the parastatal;

(b)

Additional objectives which are agreed with the management of the parastatal.

26
The financial objectives may therefore be subordinated to a number of political and social considerations, for example: 1. Service: A parastatal may be expected to provide a certain standard

of service to all customers, regardless of the fact that some individuals will receive a service at a charge well below its cost. For example, the postal service must deliver letters to remote locations for the price of an ordinary postage stamp. Social Need: The need to provide a service may be of such overriding social and political importance that the government is prepared to subsidize the industry, and accept huge losses from the industry.

There is a strong body of opinion for example, which argues that the

transport services are a social necessity and a certain level of service

must be provided, with losses made up by government subsidies

In recent years, government thinking on the issue of financial objectives in its owned parastatals and companies has assumed a different posture. This is evident in government circles with the introduction of privatization and commercialization of government enterprises. This development encourages wernment owned parastatals and companies to earn sufficient, or even surplus profits, so that the industry can provide a certain proportion, or even the entire amount of its investment needs from its own resources and possibly pay returns to investors.

Commercialization concept focuses more on profit making and profit mation while privatization emphasizes government disengagement of its hip of enterprises in favour of private individuals, corporate ations as well as the general public. However, both ideologes have as their bottom line "profit making and profit maximization". It should be noted that for every privatization, there is commercialization. In other words, commercialization means the reorganization of enterprises wholly or partly wwed by government in which such commercialized enterprises shall operate as pr making commercial venture and without subventions from the

It is hoped that government will not relent in pursuing this policy of commercialization and privatization, more so when it is a sure way of revamping anding capitalistic economy like ours. The next chapter will speak privatisation and commercialization.

COMPARISON BETWEEN THE OBJECTIVES OF COMPANIES AND STATE

OFFED ENTERPRISES

Drawing comparison between the objectives of companies and men-owned enterprises, the hallowing areas call meaningful

A company's main objective will be a financial one. The aim of mong the wealth of shareholders is too simplistic a view of what

27 this objective is, but shareholders must be provided with satisfactory return. The main objective of a state-owned enterprise is unlikely to be a financial one. company's financial objective can be expressed in terms of wealth of

A

shareholders (dividend and share value) A government-owned enterprise cannot express a financial objective in this way, but in the return on capital employed or profit/sales ratio, etc. A company's financial targets will include target for Dividends and Commuting Gearing Levels The matters which are important for

companies, are irrelevant to state-owned enterprise A company will have some non-financial objective, just as a state- owned enterprise will have some financial ones (eg to cover their operating costs, or to make a profit which will be used to provide funds to the government).

The objectives of a company will be formulated into planning target by the company's management (board of directors). In a state-owned organization, management will have less freedom of decisionmaking and many have to accept targets that are imposed on them by agreement departments and government ministers. The success or failure of a public company's financial management

will be reflected in the share price.

The same gauge of success or failure is not available for a state-owned

enterprise Although the emphasis in the use of this text will be on companies, the application of many of the subjects to public corporations should not be ignored.

THE ARGUMENT AGAINST WEALTH MAXIMIZATION

Wealth maximization is a consequence of perfect competition (which many assumptions eg free entry and exit from the market, free flow of information und in the face of imperfect modern markets today it cannot be a legitimate objective of the firm.

It is also argued that profit maximization, as a business objective was developed in the early 19th century when the characteristic feature of the business structure were sell-financing by private property and singe entrepreneurship The only aim of the single owner then was to enhance his individual wealth and personal power, which could easily be satisfied by the pride maximization objective However, in the contemporary placing of things. ownership and management are separated. In this changed business setting. owner-manager of the 19th century has been replaced by professional who has to reconcile the conflicting objectives of the parties connected business firm In this new business environment, profit maximization das unrealistic, difficult, inappropriate and immoral.

28
ARGUMENT FOR WEALTH MAXIMIZATION

There are practical reasons why managers should work in the best interest of shareholders, which eventually translate into wealth maximization. Some of these arguments are discussed below:

1. Unwanted Takeover: Hostile takeover (where management does not want the firm to be taken over) are most likely to occur when a firm's share is under-valued relative to its potential indicating poor managerial decisions. If this happens, the managers either loses their jobs or the autonomy that they had prior to the acquisition. Thus to avoid takeover, managers have an incentive to take actions which maximizes share price.

2.

Managerial Labour Market: It has been argued that the managerial labour market exerts a great deal of influence on managerial behaviour, perhaps even enough to make the agency problem unimportant and not worth worrying about. It is argued that the manager's wealth is the present value of current and future income. The better the managerial performance, as measured by share price, the greater will be the salary that the manager will command both in his present and future employment. Thus, if the capital markets (share prices) provide efficient signals concerning managerial performance, and if the managerial labour market correctly values managerial performance, then the manager's own desire for personal wealth will provide a strong incentive for him to act in the shareholder's best interests.

3.

The Threat of Firing: In companies where share ownership is

concentrated in the hands of large institutions rather than individuals, the institutional money managers have the clout, if they choose, to exercise considerable influence over firm's operations. Whereas, fragmented individual investors may be uninformed, lazy or simply "Vote with the feet" by selling shares in firms where performance is below par, the institutional investors are more likely to work actively to oust an inefficient management.

Future Financing: Other factors remaining the same, a high share price is a good sign of vote of confidence on management by the stock market. This vote of confidence is an important variable required by managers when going back to the stock market for additional finance

- both equity and debt.

HOW IS VALUE OF A COMPANY INCREASED? If a company's shares are traded on the stock market, the wealth of

shareholders is increased when the share price goes up.

What will make share prices go up? Ignoring day-to-day fluctuations in price caused by patterns of supply and demand, and ignoring fluctuations caused by "environmental" factors such as changes in interest rates, the price of a company's shares will go up on a stock market when:

(a) (b) The company makes attractive profits, which it pays out as dividends or reinvestment as retained profits in the business to achieve further profit growth and dividend growth in the future; and The company achieves its attractive profits without taking business risks and financial risks which concern shareholders, and so depress

the share price. Profits and earnings, dividends, growth prospects and risk are therefore key elements in the market valuation of the shares of a public company. The

same elements will affect the "worth" to shareholders of shares in a private

company.

THE FINANCE MANAGER'S FUNCTIONS

Maximizing the wealth of the shareholders generally implies maximizing profits consistently with long-term stability. It is often found that the greatest short-term gains must be scarified in the interest of the company's longer-term prospects. In the context of this overall objective, there are three main functions of the finance manager:

1. Investment decisions 2. Financing decisions

3. Dividend decisions

In practice, these three areas are interconnected and should not be viewed in isolation.

Investment Decision: Capital resource planning is defined as "the process of evaluating and selecting long-term assets to meet strategies" (CIMA). Investment decision involves the profitable utilization of the firm's funds especially in long term project (capital project). Because the future benefits associated with such projects are not known with certainty, investment decisions necessarily involve risk. These projects are therefore evaluated in relation to their expected return and risk, for these are the factors that ultimately determine the market value of the company. To maximize the market value of the company, the financial manager will be interested in those project with maximum returns and minimum risk. An understanding of cost of

capital, capital structure and portfolio theory is a pre-requisite here. Moreover, investment decisions involve committing funds to: (a)

Internal investment projects and the withdrawal from should they turnout to be unprofitable.

such projects

(b) (c) External investment decisions, involving the takeover of another company, or a merger. Disinvestments decisions, involving the sell-off of a part or all the business, such as an unwanted subsidiary company.

30

Financing Decisions: Capital funding planning is "the process of selecting
suitable funds to finance long-term assets and working capital" (CIMA). These assets of a
company must be financed, by share capital and reserves, long term liabilities or by short term liabilities. When a company is growing it will need additional finance from one or

more of these sources. This second major decisions deals with the mode of financing or capital

structure. If it is possible to alter the total value of the company by alteration in

the capital structure, ie a combination of equity and debt of the company, then

an optimal financing mix would exist-where the market value of the company is

The finance manager must know Where additional funds can be obtained from and at what cost,

The effect on a company's profitability and value of using any particular source of funds,

The effect on financial risk of using any particular source of fund

A company ought to be profitable, but it must be "liquid too-ie it must always have access to enough cash to make its payments to creditors and employees etc when they fall due, Financing decisions therefore include cash management and negotiating bank overdrafts.

Financial management is concerned with obtaining funds for investment.

and investing those funds profitably so as to maximize the value of the firm. It

efficient to invest at a profit, it is necessary to invest so that the profits are sufficient to re-pay investors a satisfactory, (wealth maximizing) amount of

interest or dividends If a company cannot pay interest at the market rate

demanded by lenders, the lenders will prefer to invest elsewhere on the capital

mat, where they can get this rate. There is a market "opportunity cost of

borrowed funds which a company must expect to pay for new loans. Similarly, if a company cannot make big enough profits, shareholders will be dissatisfied The company will not be able to raise funds from new of shares, because investors would not be attracted Existing orders who wish to well their shares will find that buyers who have the to invest in whatever securities they choose, will Aller a low price, and the market price of the shares will be depressed here a wide-range of shares available to them, there is a opportunity cost of equity Investors have a choice. If they can obtain a better return elsewhere,

w
i
l
l

to invest in the securities of a company Finance manager

be aware of
How investors make their decisions to buy and sell the stocks and shares of a company How banks decide whether to lend money, and at what rate of

Interest What rates of return must be paid to investors in a company to prevent them from switching the funds to other investments, and what must be paid to attract new investors

31

In other words, financial management is concerned with the financial system, sources of finance and the "opportunity cost" of the capital market.

Dividend Decisions: Ordinary shareholders expect to earn dividends, and the value of a company's share will be related to the amount of dividends that a company has been paying, and also to prospects of what the dividends might be

in the future.

Dividend decisions are also directly related to financing decisions, since retained profits are the most important source of new funds to companies. What a company pays as dividends out of profits cannot be retained in the business to finance future growth, and what profits are retained represent a withholding of dividends. If a company cannot pay dividend at a reasonable rate, investors will prefer to invest elsewhere on the capital market where they can earn returns on their investments.

Dividend decisions determines the division of earnings between payments to shareholders and reinvestment in the company. Retained earnings are one of the most significant sources of funds for financing corporate growth, but dividends constitute the cash flows that secure shareholders confidence Although both growth and dividends are desirable, these goals are in conflict with each other, a higher dividend rate means less retained earnings and consequently, slower rate of growth in future earnings and share prices. The finance manager must provide reasonable answer to this conflict.

The three decisions of the finance manager determine the value of the firm to its shareholders. To maximize this value, optimal combination of the three is important.

Additionally. Finance manager functions encompasses the following:

Acquisition Decision: This covers the valuation of shares and business and

the various methods of acquisition and merger.

Working Capital Management: This involves efficient management of stocks, liquid assets, debtors and short-term credits.

Financial Control and Reporting: Any attempt of management necessarily involves at least two steps. In the first place, a manager must have a plan of what he wishes to achieve and how he intends to achieve it. Secondly, he must exercise control. This calls for monitoring of actual events against the plan and the taking of prompt action, where necessary to ensure that actual results conform as closely as possible to plan. To aid the planning and control processes, the finance manager must supply management with regular financial reports.
In carrying out the above role, finance managers are likely to draw on a number of other disciplines, notably financial and management accounting, economics, mathematics, taxation and law.

THE FINANCE FUNCTION IN ORGANIZATION The structure of the finance function in a business organization will depend to some extent on the size and individual characteristics of the organisation. The structure of a typical company might be as follows:

Credit control and debt collection activates might be listed as a responsibility of either the financial accountant or the treasurer, depending on the company's organization.

Finance underlies all business operations. Although not a frontline role such as marketing or production, it is nevertheless of equal significance since the other activities cannot be undertaken without its support.

In many organizations in this country and elsewhere, the finance function is not distinctly separated from accounting function, the function goes by either of the two names. In large, enlightened organizations however, the accounting function is often designated as a unit within the overall finance function, thus giving the impression probably rightly that finance is not only a benader function but actually encompasses accounting. In such organizations, the bead of the function is called the Finance Director or Manager and under him are three functionaries, the Treasurer, the Chief Accountant and the Internal Auditor

While the Treasurer takes charge of all activities relating to the movement of fands between the organization and outside parties such as banking, raising funds, foreign exchange management, cash forecasting, cash management, insurance, pensions, investment of surplus cash, etc, the Chief.

Accountant is responsible for management information system, appraisal major capital expenditure projects, keeping accounting records, preparation financial statements, budgeting and budgetary control, financial analyse working capital, management, etc, so that the Finance Director will be able advise the board whether any particular project is financially viable.

Internal audit, although a related function often does not report to the Finance Director or Manager, but reports directly to the Managing Director for reasons of the need to maintain a reasonable degree of independence

from the

Finance Director/Manager whose financial activities it examine and audit However, the job of the internal audit cut across the financial activities of the

entire organization.
THE ROLE OF TREASURER There are usually four core areas of activity and responsibility for

treasury department. These are: (a)

Banking; (b) Investment of Surplus cash;

Borrowing.

(c) (d) Currency Management.

The role of the treasurer is still developing, and in broad terms, could include any corporate activities or services directly associated with banking and the financial and currency markets; e.g.:

(6) (ii) Working capital control; Funding business takeovers;

(iii) Tax planning, Obtaining insurance cover for the company's assets and activities

(iv)
(v) Pensions :

The following additional roles of treasurership can be identified
Corporate Financial Objectives (a)

(1) (ii)

Financial aims and strategies Financial and treasury policies

Financial and treasury systems.

Liquidity Management (1)

Working Capital and money transmission management ▣
Banking relationships and arrangements

(iii) Money management

Cash management and liquidity management are probably the
most.

obvious responsibilities of a treasurer. In some organization
the task is largely

one of controlling stocks debtors, creditors and bank overdraft.
In cash-rich companies, the treasurer will be heavily involved
in the investment of surplus funds to earn a good yield until
they are required again form another A good relationship with
one or more banks is desirable, so that the purpose. treasurer
can negotiate overdraft facilities or loans at reasonable
interest rate.

34
(b)

;(c)

Funding Management (1) Funding policies and procedures

(ii)

Sources of funds

Types of funds

Funding management is concerned with all forms of borrowing, and alternative sources of funds, such as leasing and factoring.

The treasurer needs to know: Where funds are available B

(11) For how long

At what interest rate

(iv) (V) Whether security would be required or not. Whether interest rate would be fixed of variable.

If a company borrows, say $10 million, even a difference of %%% of in the interest cost of the loan obtained would be worth $25,000 in interest charges each year. This might help to suggest how treasurers in large companies can justify their position and salary.

(d)

Currency Management 6) Exposure polices and procedures

Exchange dealing

ii) International Monetary Economics and Exchange Regulations

(

Currency dealings can save or cost a company considerable amounts of money, and the success or shortcomings of the corporate treasurer can have a significant impact on the profit and loss account of a company which is heavily involved in foreign trade. In currency management the treasurer is concerned with the initiation of currency transactions in the group, and with issues such as dealing controls and the management of exchange rate exposure. The methods and techniques of protecting the company from currency exposure can span one or two years or even longer, and can involve strategic decisions on whether to enter into forward contracts.

(e)

Corporate Finance
Equity Capital Management

回 Business Acquisitions and Sales (iii) Project Finance and Joint Venture

Corporate finance is concerned with matters such as raising share capital, its form (ordinary or preference, or different classes of ordinary shares, etc) obtaining a stock exchange listing, dividend policy, financial information for

management, mergers, acquisitions and business sales.

Related Subjects

Corporate Taxation

@

(ii) (iii)

Risk Management and Insurance Pension Fund Investment Management

Any borrowing can be arranged in bulk-lower interest rate.

(g)

Ay replacement can be arranged in bulk-higher interest rate.

(h)

(i) Control of cash will be recognized as a separate and significant activity, concentrating on the most efficient use of funds.

The company may be provided with more sophisticated and special financial services. Experts may be employed to specialize in particular aspects e.g. foreign exchange management, interest management, etc.

Treasury could provide an excellent training ground in finance for future

line management as its staff will need to be capable of making quick bust sound

decisions.

CONTROLLER'S FUNCTIONS

1. Planning and Control: To establish, coordinate and administer, as part of management plan for the control of

operations. This will include short-term and long-term budgeting

2.

3.

Reporting and Interpreting: To compare actual performance with

operating plans and standards and to report and interpret the results of

the operations to all levels of management and to the owners of business Tax Administration: To establish and administer tax policies and

procedure

Government Reporting: To supervise or coordinate the preparation.

of report to government agencies

Protection of Assets: To assure protection of business assets.

through internal control and internal auditing.

6.

Economic Appraisal: To appraise economic and social forces and government influences and interpret their effect upon business.

5.

CHAPTER THREE

PRIVATIZATION AND COMMERCIALIZATION

INTRODUCTION

T The term "Privatization" refers to the transfer of services and interest from the state to private enterprises. In other words, privatization emphasizes government disengagement of its ownership of enterprises in favour of private individuals, corporate organization as well as the general public

Privatization covers a number of different matters, e.g 包 Selling of nationalized concerns to private shareholders

(ii) Issue of shares traded on the Nigerian stock Exchange;

(iii) Share placement with institutional investors,

(iv) Sales of assets; [v] Joint ventures with the private sector;

(vi) Relaxing monopoly rights to allow competition; (vii) Allowing private contractors to tender for the provision of

services. The principal aim of the proponents of privatization is to improve the performance of the economy, as a whole, by competition because it is believed

that monopoly positions can lead to:

(a)

(c)

a restriction of consumers choice.

inefficiencies; (b) a lack of motivation by management and employees, and

The following reasons may be ascribed to privatization: To "Loosen the grip of the public sector and make more

efficient use

(01)

of resources by opening up areas to the play of market forces. (i) Encouraging a wider ownership of shares.

Reducing the burden on the Government as a result of the sale of assets and remove future borrowing by bodies transferred, from the public sector borrowing requirement.

Similarly encourage building societies to provide mortgage finance in place of local authority support scheme.

The counter view to privatization might encompass: (1) Question of efficiency in the public sector are not easy to determine. Consideration must be given to social benefits as well as economic

(11)

efficiency Although there may be wider share ownership, this may have little effect on control of those organizations.

Public sector bodies could obtain fund for expansion from outside the public sector and yet remain under public control. (iv) The private sector would wish to purchase only profitable assets and

serviceing the "Cinderella" items in the public sector. (v) Denationalization is disruptive in a period of recession. (vi) Disposal may be made at unrealistic prices.

;COMPETITIVE TENDERING

Competitive tendering also termed contracting-out, is one element of the present government's policy of privatization. It concerns the transfer of certain services, traditionally undertaken "in-house" to private contractors. This policy affects all areas of government, central government as well as local governments. Current examples include refuse collection, catering, cleaning. laundry and vehicle repair.

(1)

Arguments in favour of this policy include: An end to "in-house" monopoly services whose bureaucracies were

accused of satisfying their own interest rather than service recipients.

An end to restrictive labour practices and low productivity. Thereby reducing the level of grants, subsidies, taxes and government expenditure. Competition allows the possibility of periodic re-contracting by public

procurement agents; competition leads to new methods of working with more modern

(iv) equipment;

(v) successful firms in a competition are subject to the incentives and penalties inherent in the terms of a fixed price contract; Penalties can be imposed for poor quality and unreliability. (vi)

Arguments against contracting-out include:

Contracting-out can lead to increased industrial relations problems; ($\equiv$) Contractors make unrealistically low bids to obtain contracts in order to eliminate "in-house" capacity thereby making the authority dependent on a private monopoly.

Contracts can provide poor quality and an unreliable service;

fiv) Some contractors have been accused of putting profits before people, (v) Contract tendering is not coatless as funds need to be spent on both managing contracts and administering the tendering procedure. Competitive tendering, being a relatively new policy, raises a number of questions. Will, for example, efficiency gains in the Waste Disposal Board result in improved refuse collection in the district where the changes occur or will some other district gains?

What is clear is that there needs to be some improvement in the management of certain contracted-out services. It is difficult to assess whether the policy of privatization promoted by the government has achieved its objectives. Depending upon their party, politicians prefer slogan such as "tyranny of state ownership and the "vandalism" of privatization. There is little, apolitical, economic data upon which reasoned argument can be made.

PRIVATIZATION AND COMMERCIALIZATION DECREE 1988

The privatization and commercialization decree 1988 provides for the privatization and commercialization of Federal Government enterprises and other enterprises in which the Federal Government has equity-interests.

39

The decree also establishes the Technical Committee on Privatization and Commercialization (TCPC) with the objective of ensuring a thorough implementation of government's policy on commercialization and privatization of its enterprises and interests. Eighteen firms were privatized by their owner ministries prior to the

establishment of TCPC in 1988 and, as at 31st May, 1992, the TCPC has privatized 27 enterprises through public offer, one through private placemen.

and seven through sale of assets.

The control, management and composition of the board of directors of privatized enterprises shall as from the date of privatization reflect the ownership structure of the enterprises.

TECHNICAL COMMITTEE ON PRIVATIZATION AND COMMERCIALIZATION

(TCPC)

A technical committee consisting of a chairman and seven other members was appointed by the President, Commander-in-Chief of the armed Forces, drawn from both the private and public sectors of the economy to perform the following functions:

(a)

Advise on the capital restructuring needs of enterprises to be privatized or commercialized in order to ensure a good reception in the Stock Exchange Market for those to be privatized as well as to facilitate good management and independent access to the capital market.

(b)

(c)

Carry out all activities required for the successful public issues of shares of the enterprises to be privatized including the appointment of issuing house, stockbroker, solicitors, trustees, accountants and other experts to the issues.

Approach, through the appointed issuing houses, the

Securities and Exchange Commission for a fair price for each issue.

(d)

Advise the Federal Government, after consultation with the Securities and Exchange Commission and the Nigerian Stock Exchange, on the allotment pattern for the sale of the shares of the enterprises concerned as follows: Not less than 10 percent and not more than 20 percent of the total.

shares on offer shall be allocated to associations and interest.

groups such as state investment agencies, workers, trade unions,

market women organizations, universities, friendly societies, local

(1)

and community associations, provided that in the case of an over subscription not more than 1 percent of the shares on offer shall be allocated toe ach state through its investment agency. The remainder of shares not distributed in accordance with above allotment shall be sold to the public in such manner and at such amounts as may be determined by the Allotment Committee of the

40
Securities and Exchange Commission and approved by the Federal Government.

(c)

Oversee the actual sale of shares of the enterprises concerned by the issuing houses in accordance with the guidelines approved by the Federal Government.

Submit to the Federal Government from time to time, for the

purpose of approval, proposals on sale of Government Shares in such

designated enterprises with a view to ensuring a fair price and even

spread in the ownership of the shares,

(8)

Ensure the success of the privatization and commercialization exercise taking into account the need for balance and meaningful participation by Americans and foreign interests in accordance with the relevant laws.

(4)

Ensure the updating of the accounts of all commercialized enterprises with a view to assuring financial disciple.

The Technical Committee shall perform such other functions as may be assigned to it, from time to time, by the President, Commander-in-Chief of the Armed Forces. Whenever the Technical Committee is of the view that any enterprise is not suitable for disposal by public issue of shares, the Technical Committee shall recommend to the Federal Government the mode of disposal of such enterprise. The Technical Committee shall seek and obtain the prior approval of the Federal Government for the price of any share issue in respect of any designated enterprise and the pattern of its allotment.

INCORPORATION OF ENTERPRISE TO BE PRIVATIZED

The Technical Committee shall, not later then 12 months after the commencement of the Decree, incorporate into limited liability companies under the Companies and Allied Matters

Decree, 1990 all enterprises to be privatized where such enterprises are not already incorporated. Without prejudice to the generality of the incorporation clause, the Federal Government, acting on the advice of the Technical Committee, may direct that any enterprise affected by the Decree shall not be incorporated into a public limited liability company in view of its weak financial structure but that the operations of such enterprise shall be wound-up and its assets disposed by sale or in any other manner approved by the Federal Government.

OFFER OF SALE AND MODE OF SALE OF PRIVATIZED ENTERPRISES All shares of enterprises to be privatized under the decree shall be offered

for sale in the Nigerian Capital Market. All offers for sale of the shares shall be by public issues except when the Federal Government, on the advice of the Technical Committee, decides that the shares of any affected enterprises should be sold by private placement.

41
ALLOTMENT OF SHARES OF PRIVATIZED ENTERPRISES Not less than 10 percent and not more than 20 percent of the t

shares on offer shall be allotted to associations and interest groups such not limited, to state investment agencies, workers, trade unions, market w organizations, universities, friendly societies, local and community associate provided that in the case of an over-subscription not more than 1 percent of

share on offer shall be allotted to each state through its investment agency The remainder of shares not distributed in accordance with the abo provision shall be sold to the public in such manner and at such amounts may be determined by the Allotment Committee of the Securities and Exchange

Commission and approved by the Federal Government. The allotment of shares as above mentioned shall give priority subscriptions by workers and management as well as non-management of the particular enterprises to be privatized.

Not more than 10 percent of the shares of offer shall be reserved for the staff of the company, and in the case of the over-subscription, no individual enterprise

shall, be allowed to hold more than 1 percent equity in anyone COMMERCIALIZATION OF GOVERNMENT ENTERPRISES

"Commercialization means the re Organization of enterprises wholly partly owned by the Federal Government in which such commercialize enterprises shall operate as profit-making commercial ventures and wither.

subventions from the Federal Government.

Among government enterprises slated for commercialization are Nigeria Hotels Limited, Aba Textile Mills, National Cargo Handling Limited, Nigeria Food Co Ltd, and other enterprises mentioned in Part 1 of Schedule 2 of the Decree shall be fully privatized, te. 100% of equity held by the Federal Government are fully shed out. Railway Corporation, Airport Authority, National Electric Power Authority etc shall be partially commercialized Enterprises slated for full commercialization are NNPC, NITEL NICON, Re-Insurance Corporation, Mining Corporations Coal Corporation, Ports Authority, etc.

INTERPRETATION

Privatization and Commercialization Decree 1988 Decree NO, 9.25 Official Gazette No. 42 Vol. 75 of 6th July. 1988, gave the following official

interpretation.

"Commercialization" means the reorganization of enterprises wholly a partly owned by the Federal Government in which such Commercialize Enterprises shall operate as profit-making commercial ventures and without subventions from the federal government.

"Enterprises" means any corporation board, company or parastate established by or under any enactment in which the Federal Government, any of its Departments, Ministries or agencies has ownership or equity interest

42

and shall include a partnership, joint venture or any other form of venture or any other form of business arrangement or organization.

"Privatization" means the relinquishment of part or all of the equity and other interest held by the Federal Government or its agency in enterprises whether wholly or partly owned by the Federal Government.

CONCLUSION

The moves to encourages the public sector to behave more like the private sector helped to break down a number of barriers. But these pressures have become more insistent and more political in recent years, as those who believe that the public sector is chronically inefficient have moved to the canter of the political stage. Such people have maintained with increasing vehemence that the only way to remedy the position is to transfer the provision of services where at all possible to the private sector and that what remains in the public sector should follow private sector financial and management practices.

The recent history of privatization policy must be classified as one that

has followed no consistent rationale. The transfer of ownership per se provides

no clear path to increased efficiency.

3.

A bill of exchange enables the debtors to postpone payment to the date of maturity.

4. A bill is a proof of the indebtedness of the debtor to the creditor A bill of exchange may also be used in a tripartite transaction with credit Eg. Sandra Eric in Washington, USA sold goods for $50,000 to Lucas Chen in New York, payment to be made in dollars. Sandra Eric owes Becky Johnson in London $50,000. He draws a bill of exchange on Lucas Chen payable to Becky Johnson (Fig. 3). If Lucas Chen accepts the bill Becky Johnson may keep it till 1 April when it will mature and demand payment from Lucas Chen. In the alternative, Becky may discount the bill at a bank or discount house before 1" April or she may endorse it over to pay any debt which she owes.

5.

NOTING FEE

This is the fee paid by the drawer or holder to a notary public (who must be a legal practitioner) to note and protest the dishonour of a foreign bill. The noting fee, being a charge to be borne by the drawee (i.e. the debtor) will be passed on to him, through book entry, by the drawer or holder.

DISCOUNTING OF BILLS OF EXCHANGE Where the drawer (i.e. the creditor) chooses the option to discounting the

bill, he would take it to a bank or discount house and obtain a loan for a term not extending beyond the maturity date of the bill. The bill would be negotiated (L.e. transferred) to the bank or discount house, and in exchange, he would receive an amount, which will be less than the value of the bill. The difference

known as discounting charge is the finance charge of the bank or discount

house on the facility granted. At the maturity date, the bank or discount house

would collect the full value of the bill from the debtor. In the event of the debtor dishonouring the bill, the bank would debit the account of the creditor with the full value of the bill. When he is notified, the creditor would pass the appropriate entry by debiting the debtor's account and crediting the bank account.

It should be noted that the debtor has nothing to do with the discounting charge. The charge must be borne by the holder or drawer, debiting the profit and loss account and crediting the bills receivable account.

Discounted Bills: When a holder of a bill decides to sell the bill at price lower

than the value, usually to a bank or discount house, the instrument eventually becomes a discounted bill. When the bill matures and the drawee pays the amount due, then it becomes a Retired Bill.

DISHONOURED BILLS

A bill is said to be dishonoured when it is presented for payment of maturity, the drawee, for one reason or the other, fails to pay the amount due When this happens, the drawee becomes either a debtor again or a bad debt t be written off.

60
A bill may be dishonoured by non-acceptance or by non-payment.

Dishonoured by Non-Acceptance: When a bill is dully presented for

acceptance and is not accepted with the customary time, the person presenting

it must treat it as dishonoured by non-acceptance. If he does not, the holder shall lose his right of recourse against the drawer and endorsers. A bill is dishonoured for non-acceptance ar

When it is duly presented for acceptance, and acceptance is refused cannot be obtained, or where an advice is sent through the post office, and acceptance is not obtained within ten days from the time the advice.

is posted. When presentment for acceptance is excused and the bill is not accepted.

b)

When a bill is dishonoured by non-acceptance an immediate right of recourse against the drawer and endorsers accrues to holders and no presentment for payment is necessary. The holder of a bill may refuse to take a qualified acceptance, and if he

does not obtain an unqualified acceptance, may treat the bill as dishonoured by non-acceptance.

Dishonoured b Non-Payment: A bill is dishonoured by non-payment When it is duly presented to payment and payment is refused or cannot

be obtained or, where an advice is sent through the post office, and payment is not obtained: (1) in the case of a fixed determinable future date bill, before the date the bill falls due in case of a bill payable on demand, within ten days from the time

the advice is posted. When presentment is excused and the bill is overdue and unpaid.

(b)

When a bill is dishonoured by non-payment, an immediate right of recourse against the drawer and endorsers accrues to the holder.

EFFICIENT STOCK CONTROL & FINANCING

Efficient stock control though not a real source of finance, but a redaction in excessive stocks consumption and stock wastages can reduce the need for finance and so would achieve a saving in finance. Meticulous observance of minimum and maximum stock levels, re-order quantity, re-order level, lead time, and other relevant stock control measures will at as a catalyst towards effective cost control and reduction thereby enhancing the financial Position of the company. Implementation of standard cost card, acquisition of high quality stock of raw materials, efficient inspection and reception of material as well as good storage facility and procedures for material will also go

4 long way in saving the Bases of V by extension boo Smarty inventory financing generally involves borrowing funds

avesty as seventy Inventory is an attractive form of security beca markable and it can wally be sold a prices which are higher than valee Although aventories may exist in different meg a man wwwk-in-progress and finished goods, only finished goods and row m may be acceptable to lender as security All types of goods would not deally the use as security Goods which are durable, of high value in relacion se and which are not too specialed that is which have applicans so as to facilitate sale in the event of default would be prelemed For the same reasons goods which are perishable, of relatively little value in relative to sue and which have very specialized uses, would not be very acceptable as security

TYPES OF LIEN

lender can either take a general for floating len or a specific len the inventory Where he opts for a specific len, he can again decide either to magistrst receipt goods held in borrower's warehouse or custody) against a warehese recept goods held in leader's warehouse or a warehouse owned and agement by an independent third party). The mode fa operating these fems of security is described below

2

BORROWING AGAINST A GENERAL OR FLOATING LIEN: This involves using the total inventory held by a firm (which may comprise a miscellany of items) as security for a short-term loan. The stock position is normally relatively Said since goods customarity move in and out of stocks on a continuing basis. The lender's Sen "fixes" in the event of defeat on the goods actually held in stock at the material time. The lender is at great risk unless the inventory held at any one time is at least equal to the value of the loan. It is for this reason that the amount loaned against this security is customarily low seldom higher than 50 to 60% of the value of the inventory. The lender also usually carries out periodic inspections of the inventory during the term of the loan - in order to ensure that it is not depleted below an acceptable level Typically, only business which maintain a fairly stable level of inventories are able to raise loans on the basis of a general or floating len

BORROWING AGAINST TRUST RECEIPT: A trust receipt is an acknowledgement executed by the borrower to the effect that it holds specified goods in trust fer the lender for the duration of the loan. The procedure for operating this leam is thus The finance company or commercial bank pays for goods which are delivered to the borrower's warehouse. Borrower

delivers a trust receipt, which specifically identifies and describes these goods to the lender. Borrower may however sell the goods provided that he immediately thereafter applies the proceeds to defray the loan plus accrued interest. The lender thereupon releases the
lien on the goods disposed of. The essence of this arrangement is that the goods legally belong to the lender for as long as the loan remains unsettled. A trust receipt loan is appropriate when the goods in question

have small individual values and the turnover is fairly rapid. Trust

receipt agreements normally give the lender the right to visit the

borrower's warehouse from time to time to inspect the goods and to call

for periodic inventory reports attesting to the existence, value and

satisfactory condition of the goods held in trust.

BORROWING AGAINST WAREHOUSE RECEIPT: Where the nature and volume of the goods permit and the lender seeks greater protection against risks, he may insist on lending on a warehouse receipt. A warehouse receipt is an acknowledgement by the lender's own warehouse or agent (usually an independent third party in the form of a public warehouse) to the effect that goods of a specified identity, volume and description are held in stock as security for a loan given by the lender. The distinctive feature here is that the warehouse is either owned or controlled by the lender and will act only on its express instruction, Consequently, the goods are released only when the lender receives part or full repayment of the loan. It should be noted that the lender's warehouse need not necessarily always reside in the lender's own premises nor for that matter, does he need to own or manage a warehouse of his own. As already pointed out the leader may appoint an independent warehousing business to act for him. Under certain conditions e.g. high transportation cost, borrower's convenience in terms of operational logistics, etc, the lender may lease space in the borrower's own warehouse or set up a tent shed in the latter's premises. A suitable demarcation of such space with a rope or fence and the appointment of his own warehouse personnel would be all that is needed to satisfy the conception of lender's warehouse.

The cost of borrowing against warehouse receipt is considerably more than that of a trust receipt. Apart from the interest payable under the loan balances, the administrative cost of running the warehouse and the insurance cost of the inventory are also ultimately borne by the borrower. Consequently, unless the volume of operations is large enough to absorb these costs conveniently this form of financing will not be justified. The facility of borrowing against warehouse receipt is not customarily available to the small firm.

PLEDGING OF ACCOUNTS RECEIVABLE This involves the use of accounts receivable (debtors) as collateral for a

loan. In some countries, the credit system has become very highly developed to the point where some commercial banks as well as specialized finance companies would normally accept accounts receivable as security for a short- term loan. This line of business is however highly specialized and requires the best system of credit evaluation.

63

The procedure followed is that both lender and the firm have to agree on the specific debts to be used as collateral Not all the book debts would quality for use. Acceptable debts are usually those owing by customers of relatively good credit standing, that is, who pay regularly and are seldom in default Against the debts would be acceptable only during the normal duration of credit. For instance, where a particular customer is normally given 30 days. I the debt has become due but is still unpaid, it could no longer serve as acceptable collateral. The amount, which a lender is willing to advance on the security of a debt, is also usually substantially less than the face value of the debt. And allowance is usually made for the possibility that the customer may subsequently return some of the goods purchased or claim some form of rebates on account, say, of quality and specification etc. These when they do occur have the effect of reducing the effective debt. Allowance is also made for the eventuality that some of the debt may not be fully recoverable. Consequently, the value advanced on each debt may vary from 50 to 80% of its book value.

The loan terms usually specify that the money advanced should be repaid as soon as the debts are collected but at any event no later than their due date, that is, when the credit term granted the customer expires. This source of finance is therefore extremely short-term since it covers only the period of credit normally granted to customers. The loan must be repaid once the period of credit expires, notwithstanding that the particular customer has not actually settled his debt. This condition further makes it imperative, at least from the stand point of the firm, that only debts of high quality are pledged. If this is not so, the repayment of loan could impose very severe strain. The lender of course also has equal interest that the transaction is successfully concluded and to this end would usually devote considerable effort, through detail investigation and analysis of borrower's accounts receivables records, to seeing that the debts to be pledged are carefully selected.

As already noted, a one-shoot action to pledge accounts receivables may bring an extremely short-term financial relief to the firm. In other to extend such relief over a longer period, however, the action may be repeated continuously. In this situation a somewhat permanent relationship is established with lender whereby all new credit transactions are evaluated on a continuing basis and loans taken against them until they are settled, whereupon the loans are discharged, and new loans taken and the cycle continues. Accounts receivable pledging thus becomes a semi-permanent source of financing working capital. It is not usual for credit customers to be formally notified of the fact that their debts are being used as security for a loan, since this may led to some misunderstanding of the financial standing of the firm, and in any case pledging does not create direct relationship between them and the lender. This is not to say however that some customers would not know of the arrangement, but it seems that any ensuing harm can be contained as long as such knowledge is kept within manageable limits.

The interest cost of loans secured with accounts receivables is ironically normally higher than the interest on unsecured bank loan by 2 or 3 percent. The reason for this is the additional administrative work, which it entails. These comprise principally the continuous routine investigation of customer

circumstances as well as the continuous monitoring of borrower's accounts receivables records and the reconciliation of the loan account.

FACTORING

Factoring is a service that does not have a concise definition. However a meaningful and intelligent attempt was made to attach a definition to it by the International Institute for the Unification of Private Law thus:

"Factoring is...a contract by which the factor is to provide at least two of

the services (finance, the maintenance of accounts, the collection of accounts

receivable and protection against credit risks) and the suppliers is to assign to the factor on a continuing basis, by way of sales or security accounts receivable

arising from the sale of goods... or services". (1983) Factoring is therefore a source of short-term finance and also a means of managing and controlling debtors. Factoring is a financial and administrative service designed to relieve management of certain routine financial matters, thus freeing management time for other activities.

A factor is defined as doer or transactor of business for another, but a factoring organization specializes in trade debts of a client (business customer) on the client's behalf. Simply, a debt factor is a finance house, in some cases also a commercial bank, which specializes in purchasing trade debts and collecting them for a commission. The sale of debts is a special welcome facility for those businesses, which are compelled by the nature of their industry to give fairly long periods of credits to their customers and suppliers.

There are three main aspects of factoring:

Administration of the clients invoicing, sales accounting and debt

collection service.

(a)

(b) Credit protection for the client debts whereby the factor takes over the risk of loss from bad debts and so "insures" the clients against such losses. This service is also referred to as "debts underwriting" or the

"purchase of a client debts". (1) The factor usually purchases these debts "without recourse" to the

client which means that in the event that the clients customers are unable to pay what they owe, the factor will not ask for his money back from the client. (ii) Not every factoring organisation will purchase approved debts without recourse and "without recourse" factoring might be

provided especially in cases where the sizes of the debts are

particularly high, or the factor would not approve the debt for a

"without recourse" agreement.

(c) Making payment to client in advance of collection of debts. This might be referred to as "factor finance" because the factor is providing case to the client as a pre-payment of outstanding debts. There is a separate charging structure for debt administration and the "cash in advance" service. The cash in advance service is not always asked for by the client.

The risk which a debt factor takes is much greater than that associated with the pledging of debts, since the debt factor assumes full responsibility the collection of the debts as well as for any portions which rema unrecoverable. In order to minimize this risk, the factor generally applies very strict criteria for selection of debt that it will accept to purchase. Where company usually factors its debts, the selection criteria employed by the facton generally influence the company's own credit policy. In some cases, company's factor would even accept to manage the company's credit policy on the latter's behalf so as to ensure that every credit which is extended automatically accepted for purchase by the factor.

The debt factor collects directly from the company's debtors. It is therefore imperative that the debtors are informed of the factoring arrangements and in fact instructed that they should effect settlement direct to the factor. Any collections of factored debts, which for any reason come into the hands of the company, are moneys due to the factor. A usual feature of factoring contracts is the NON-RECOURSE provision. This stipulates that the factor cannot recover from the company in the event of the debtor being unable to pay. The possibility of loss through had debt is part of the risk which the factor assumes.

The factoring of debts strictly speaking does not entitle the company to receive payment in advance of the normal due date for collection, that is at the expiration of the credit period. It should be noted that what the company pays is a commission and not interest. Consequently, the factoring facility is mainly a transfer of the responsibility for debt collection and strictly speaking not necessarily one of obtaining a temporary accommodation for the duration of the credit. Sometimes, however, factoring contract provides for a situation where the company can obtain an advance against the factored debts before the normal due date. Where this occurs, interest at a specified rate or market ruling rate is usually payable for period of the accommodation. Subject to this arrangement however, the company is normally entitled to the benefit of any early settlement by debtors.

The commission paid for debt factoring is usually between 2 and 3 percent of the book value of the debt.

DEBTS ADMINISTRATION SERVICE IN FACTORING

(a)

(b)

(c)

The administration of a client's debts by the factor covers: Keeping the books of account for sales, i.e. a book-keeping service for the

sales ledger;

Sending out invoices to customers;

Collection of the debts;

(d) Credit control (ensuring that customers pay on time etc).

The factor takes on the debt administration service from the issue of the invoice. The client company must of course create the invoices and will usually mail them direct to the customer, and send a copy to the factor. The factor will then post the invoice to the sales ledger account of the customers.

66

Occasionally, a client firm may send the invoices to the factor who then mails them to the client's customers.

For the client, the advantages are: The factor takes on the job for debt administration, which saves staff cost

1. for the client.

2. The factor performs the service economically, by taking advantage of economies of scale for a large debt administration organization. This enables the factor to price his services reasonably.

3. The factor's service fee for debt administration varies according to the size of the client's operation and the factor's risk. A factor is unlikely to agree to provide a service to small firms, firms in a high-risk market or with a history of bad debts, or to businesses selling small value items to the general public.

CREDIT PROTECTION (DEBT UNDERWRITING) IN FACTORING

Factors have an information system of credit intelligence, and can assess credit risks of a client's customers and advice the client accordingly. Clients can make use of the factor's credit management services which are "of a standard that few could or would provide for themselves" (John Lenton: the Bankers Magazine, March 1981).

Most factors provide a debt administration service in which credit protection is an integral part. This is because the service is usually without recourse to the client in the event of non-payment by the customers. The factor will be willing to provide credit protection to the client but only if it can also apply its own credit control procedures i.e. it will only protect the client against bad debts if it has been able to approve the granting of credit in the first place. The factor will do this is one of two ways:

Carry out credit checks for individual customer orders; In the case of regular customers of the client, set a credit limit for that customers. The client does not then have to apply for approval of credit sales, provided that the customer remains within his credit limit. (b)

(a)

WITHOUT RECOURSE factoring virtually means that the factor buys the client's debts from him and so the client is guaranteed credit protection against bad debts. It is important to realize, however, that a factor is not a debt collection agency in the sense that he can be relied on to get money out of

customers when no one else can. Factors are involved in normal debt administration (bookkeeping, invoicing and credit management as well as collecting money) and so do not

want to get involved with problem customers. Under a without recourse arrangement, the factor assumes full to individual

responsibility for the credit control because he bears the credit risk. (a) The factor will approve the amount of credit allowed

customers by the client. (b) The factor will keep a continuous watch over the customer's account. (c) If a customer becomes overdue with a payment, the factor will consult with the client. The client may decide to take over the bad debt risk from

the factor, rather than incur bad will from the customer if the factor we to take legal action to recover the debt. Otherwise the factor would free to take non-payers to court to obtain payment.

WITH RECOURSE Factoring, the client bears the bad debt risk, not the factor. However, even in the case of with recourse factoring the client may ask the factor to assess the credit worthiness of customers since the factor handling the sales ledger and debt collection arrangements.

The most important aspect of this operation, however, is the initial assessment of a customer as a credit risk, and it is in this area that a factoring organization should be able to provide a quality of service based on their credit rating expertise that the clients could not achieve by themselves.

MAKING ADVANCES ON DEBTS (FACTORING)

A factor organization might be asked by a chent to advance funds to the client against the security of the debts which the factor has purchased, up to 80% of the value of the debt. For example, if a client makes credit sales of $100,000 per month, the factor would be willing to advance up to 80% of the invoice value (here $80,000.00), in return for a commission charge, and interest will be charged on the amount of funds advanced. The rate of interest would be tied to bank base rate, and will possibly be a little higher than the client would pay for a bank overdraft. The balance of the money will be paid to the client when the customers have paid the factor, or after an agreed period.

This service gives the client immediate cash in place of a debt (which is a promise of cash in the future). If the client needs money to finance operations. borrowing from a factor against trade debts is therefore an alternative to asking a bank for an overdraft, although, they will probably charge higher interest. Whereas a bank overdraft would be shown in the client's balance sheet as a current liability, factor financing does not appear in the client's balance sheet at all. Hence factoring is a form of off-balance sheet finance.

If we return to the example of the client with monthly turnover of $100,000, who obtains an advance of 80% of invoiced debts from the factor, let us suppose that the client's debtors normally take 2 months to pay, and the factor charges interest at 15% per annum on the amount advanced.

(a) Before factor financing arrangement, the client would have receive $100,000 per month, or $1,200,000 per annum from debtors. With the factor financing arrangement, the client will also receive a regular $1,200,000 per annum (less the factor charges) except that there will be an initial advance of 2 months x $80,000 $160,000 in cash when the arrangement begins. Every subsequent month, the factor will then pay the $20,000 balance due from the debts when the customers pay plus a further advance of $80,000, the annual interest charge would therefore be $160,000 x 15% $24,000. (b)

Advances from a factor are particularly useful for rapidly growing companies that need more and more cash to expand their businesses quickly,

68
by purchasing more stocks and allowing more credit sales than they would otherwise be able to.

FACTORING IN NIGERIA

boin Although, it is useful for students to understand the principles of factoring, this is not a very important source of short term finance for Nigerian companies for now, considering the level of our development. Besides, a large number of Nigeria companies sell goods to government and government agencies. Given the poor payment record of government agencies, finance.

companies are reluctant to provide factoring services in respect of these debts. Nevertheless, since the deregulation of the domestic economy with the introduction of the second-tier foreign exchange market, a number of finance companies have sprung up particularly in Lagos and other major towns and cities. These companies are offering various types of financial services

including factoring.

THE CHARGES FOR FACTORING

The charges for factoring are usually a three-part tariff. Interest on finance that is advanced against invoices. Factors make their profit by charging interest at a higher rate than their own cost of borrowing from their bank. (a)

(b) (c)

A fee for the sales ledger and credit protection services. Additional fee for "one-off" services such as suing bad debtors in the case of with recourse factoring..

EXAMPLE 1

Nation Limited makes annual credit sales of $1,500,000. Credit terms are 30 days, but its debt administration has been poor and the average collection period has been 45 days with %% of sales resulting in bad debts which are written off.

A factor would take on the task of debts administration and credit checking, at an annual fee of 25% of credit sales. The company would save $30,000 per annum in administration costs. The payment period would be 30 days. The factor would also provide and advance 80% of invoiced debts at an interest rate of 14% (3% over the current prime rate).

The company can obtain an overdraft facility to finance its debtors at a rate of 24% over the prime rate.

Required:

Should the factor's services be accepted, on consideration of cost alone? Assume a constant monthly sales turnover.

SOLUTION

It is assumed that the factor would advance an amount equal to 80% of the invoiced debts, and the balance 30 days later.

69

debt colle

(a) The current situation is as follows, using the company's staff and a bank overdraft to finance all debts.

Credit Sales

$1,500,000 per annum

Average Credit Period Cost of Credit Financed by O/D:

Interest

45 days

$
45 x $1,500,000 x 134%

24,966

7,500

365

Bad Debts=4% x $1,500,000

Total Cost

32,466

The cost of a factor

Credit sales financed by the factor

= 80% x 1,500,000 $1,200,000.

For consistent comparison, we must assume that 20% of credit sak must be financed by bank overdraft.

Average Credit period now

30 days

Cost of factoring:

30

$
Factor finance Interest

x $1,200,000 x 14% =

x $300,000 x 134% =

2%% x $1,500,000

13,808

Overdraft interest

365 30

3,329

17,137

365

Cost of factor service

37,500

Administration cost savings Net Cost of Factor

Recommendation: The factor is cheaper, more efficient at

(30,000) 24.637

debts collection hence should be accepted.

EXAMPLE 2

The sales ledger of UNIRON Agencies Limited contains the names of five

debtors James, John, Zeb, Simon and Peter with outstanding debt balance of $2,400, $3,200. $2,000, $1,200 and $1,200 respectively. The debts are dur within 30, 20, 50, 40 and 30 days in that order.

EMESONS (Nig.) Limited has agreed to factor the debts at the cost of 2 of the aggregate debts. This means that EMESONS Limited would pay the full 100% of the invoiced amounts on the agreed average maturity date. Under the arrangement, the factor, in addition to the organizational

function, agrees to advance up to 80% of the invoiced value to the client as soon

(b)

as the invoice is raised and the credit worthiness of the customer is established When the debt matures and is paid, the factor remits to his client the balance 20% less the service charge and the interest payment. Assume a ten-day interest rate of 0.5% on a normal credit period of 60

days.

Calculate

Average payment date

The interest charge payable by client. The service charge payable by client.

14)

1 Total payment by factor to client.

Total charge payable by client. Maturity payment by factor to client.

Due

SOLUTION

Average Payment Date

Debtors

Invoiced Amount (2)

24

Within

(4)-2x3

James

John

2,400

3,200

30 days

20 days

72,000

64,000

Zeb

2,000

50 days

Simon

Peter

1,200

1.200

40 days

48,000

36.000

30 days

320,000

10,000

320,000

Average payment date- -32 days 10,000

Workings Using the future value interest formula

EV- 07 where 0.005, - 000057 1.0304

6

The future value interest rate to be applied dly by factor in 00304 or 3.04% the money pa

71

MERITS OF FACTORING

Improved credit control, reduced debt collection periods, reduced bad

debts and makes for better assessment of risk.

There is also a savings in administrative costs because the cost of hiring

the factor will be relatively less than the personnel and other costs

necessary for maintaining the sales ledger. More time is released for the entrepreneur to develop other

3 business

aspects of the

The financing function improves the liquidity and cash flows of the firm and consequently encourages growth. Because of the improved liquidity, discounts can be taken on purchases more easily while the firm's credit rating will also improve.

DEMERITS OF FACTORING

There is the danger of losing the confidence (patronage) of some

customers who may have the erroneous impression that the use of

factor is an indication that the firm is having flow problems. Factors are often too selective about the businesses they associate with. For instance, firms that have seasonal trading pattern or sell to large number of small customers may not be able to attract the services of the

factor, their genuine needs not withstanding 3. New firms and others in the service sector may be considered too risky by

the factor.

Besides, the firm must be relatively sound with reasonable sales figures, to be acceptable to the factor.

INVOICE DISCOUNTING

Invoice discounting is related to factoring and many factors will provide an invoice discounting services. Invoice discounting is the purchase of a selected invoices at a discount by a factor or invoice discounter. The invoice discounter does not take over the administration of the client's sales ledger, and the arrangement is purely for the advance of cash. A client should only want to have some invoices discounted when he has a temporary cash shortages, and so invoice discounting tends to consist of "one-off deals".

If a chent needs to generate cash he can approach a factor or invoice discounter, who will offer to purchase selected invoices and advance up to 75% of their value. At the end of each month, the factor or invoice discounter will Pay over the balance of the purchase price, less charges, on the invoices that have been settled in the month

Receipts from the paid invoices belong to the invoice discounter or factor. There is an element of credit protection in the invoice discounting services, but it real purpose is to improve the client's cash flow and cash position. Since the factor or invoice discounter does not control debt administration and relies on the chent to collect the debts for him, it is a more risky operation than factoring proper and so a factor might only agree to offer an invoice discount services to reliable, reputable, credit-worthy and well established companies.

73

Invoice discounting has not been a very significant source of finance for Americans and Europe companies for the same reasons that factoring has not gained prominent grounds. It is hoped that with time, the economy will create an enabling environment for factoring and invoice discounting to flourish.

HIRE PURCHASE

A hire purchase transaction is one in which the seller of an item parts with possession and transfers same to a buyer who, in return pays to the seller an amount known as hire purchase price by way of an initial deposit plus periodic installments over the hire period. The hire purchase price will normally be higher than the normal selling price of the item, the difference being hire purchase interest (or finance charge).

It should be noted that what the hire purchase buyer has while the hire period lasts is just possession. He does not acquire title until he has paid the last installment and exercise his option to acquire title by paying a further token sum which shall be stipulated in the hire purchase agreement. The hire purchase buyer however has the first option and the item cannot be sold to another person unless he has indicated his willingness to exercise the option.

Hire purchase price is the total sum (deposit plus installments) payable by the hirer, while cash price, which is normally lower than the hire purchase price, is the normal selling price or market price of the goods. Hire purchase interest, also known as finance charge is the excess of the hire purchase price over the cash price. The hire purchase interest is the compensation to the seller for having his funds tied down with the buyer over the hire period: Deposit is the initial sum payable by the hirer at the inception of the hire purchase transaction.

Hire purchase is a means whereby the hiree allows the hirer to receive goods, items or assets for other than an immediate cash payment, except initial deposit, however, various financial arrangement may be made. The goods remain the property of the hiree (supplier) and the hirer (customer) pays installments over a stipulated period at the end of which he pays a further amount, termed an option to purchase, which then gives him ownership. Under a hire purchase agreement the customer obtains possession of the goods at the outset.

A Industrial hire purchase, or installment credit, is a method of payment for plant and machinery out of income rather than capital. Use of the equipment is gained on payment of the first installment. Although it is relatively expensive, it leaves other sources of finance free for emergencies and, in contrast to bank overdrafts. The cost is fixed at the outset and will not be affected by changes in money market conditions. The repayment period will rarely be greater than two years, which in most cases will be shorter than the useful life of the asset acquired.

A number of finance companies in Nigeria provide hire purchase finance for the purchase of cars or trucks. Perhaps, the best known being Benthworth Finance (BFN). The finance companies usually raise bank credit to transact their own operations. In the alternative, promissory notes issued by the

74

purchaser of the vehicle may be discounted with banks, insurance companies and other investors in the money market. The hirer takes possession and usage of the asset while the hiree retains

title of ownership until the hirer exercise the option to purchase which eventually transfers ownership to him. if the hirer defaults in payment of instalment charges during the period of the agreement the hiree can repossess the asset and the hirer will loose all previous install mental payments to the point of default. Although the hirer does not have the legal ownership of the assets during the period of the agreement, he is permitted to show the assets in his books and to claim capital allowance on them. Besides, the interest payable is an allowable expense for corporation tax purposes.

The disadvantage, however, is that it is an expensive source of funds. Besides, until the last payment as well as option to purchase is made the assets cannot be as security for further borrowing. Smaller firms who would have been denied access to medium term funds

on account of their small size, reduce their liquidity problem through hire purchase arrangement.

FINANCING OF RETAIL SALES BY HIRE PURCHASE

A retailer selling goods on install mental credit may be able to reduce strain on his own financial resources by arranging a hire purchase arrangement directly between the customer and a financial company. The finance company will pay the retailer the cash price for the goods but may require him either to guarantee the transaction or to re-purchase the goods if the customer defaults. Alternatively, the retailer may enter into hire purchase agreements with his customer and then, using a process know as "Block Discounting" sell the debts to a finance company for immediate payment at an agreed percentage say 75% of their collection value.

CHAPTER FIVE

INTRODUCTION

SOURCES OF LONG TERM FINANCE

Long-term finances are funds used essentially for financing long term projects like buildings, plants, premises, equipment, machinery, vehicles projects have life span of more than one year. To this end, long-term finances are funds that remain with the company for operational activities either on a permanent basis or for a relatively long period of time usually more than one year A company must also plan for the size, type and use of long-term funds just as it is done for short-term finance. This is because lack of proper planning and proper matching of the type of funds employed with the project so financed may lead to high cost of financing and inadequate matching of revenues generated by such projects with the maturities of the funds. The assets of a business must be financed somehow, and when a business is growing, the

additional assets must be financed by additional capital. Finance, whether short-term or long-term, can be referred to as a resource, which can be bought and sold in a market in very much the same manner as the raw materials of a manufacturing process. The analogy can be continued further, for, just as there are different types and qualities of materials which may be bought at different prices in different markets, so there are several different sources of finance each with their individual characteristics. Again, just as the manufacturer of a product will require a particular

blend of materials of different types, so efficient financing will require an appropriate combination of capital from the available sources. A finance manager will need and expert knowledge of these if he is to use them to the best advantage of the company. Long-term funds are usually sourced from the capital market.

Capital structure refers to the way in which an organization is financed, by a combination of long-term capital (ordinary shares and reserves, preference

MATCHING ASSETS WITH FUNDS shares, loan capital such as debentures, bank loans, convertible loan stock, etc.) and short-term funds/liabilities such as bank overdraft, creditors etc. This is amply demonstrated when a look is taken at the balance sheet of any company.

It is often considered prudent that assets, which "pay back" profits over a long period of time, should be financed by long term funds (equity or debt). In this way, the returns made by the asset will be sufficient to pay either the interest cost of the loans raised to buy it, or dividends on its equity funding. Simply put, long-term capital should be used to finance long term project. If on the other hand, a long-term asset (project) is financed by short-term funds, the company cannot be certain that when thee loan becomes repayable, it will have enough cash (from profits) to do so. Although short-term borrowing (usually from banks) can be arranged or renewed so as to become longer term, there will

79

always be risks that the loan may be cancelled, or not renewed, or that interest rates will rise, or government credit control policies become tougher etc. Inability to repay the loan, even though the asset is profitable, might under such circumstances force a company into liquidation. To save the company from "untimely death through liquidation,

occasioned by unmatching assets financing and to enhance the going concern status of the organization, it is usually prudent not to finance all of its short term assets with short term funds (liabilities). By and large, short-term assets should be financed partly with short term funding and partly with long-term capital. This development will boost the cash and liquidity position of the company.

Long-term finance, therefore include the following:

INTERNAL FINANCE (RETAINED EARNINGS) Naturally, it is not an overstatement to mention that companies (private

or public) are in business with a view to profiting. This internally generated finance (profit), through operational activities, plays an important role as a source of long-term funds to companies. It should be remembered that profits generated by companies are usually apportioned among three interested parties. Out of it, shareholders receive dividende, out of it still, tax liability is settled to the government and finally as retained earnings, which constitute internally generated finance. Retained earnings are kept by the company by way of reserves or immediately plough back into investments for the purpose of growth and expansion. Interestingly, it should be noted that retained earnings remain permanent with the organization. The size of retained earnings is a reflection of the size of the profits earned; hence it is advisable for companies to work assiduously hard for a continuous improvement on their profitability drive.

ORDINARY SHARE CAPITAL (EQUITY)

Ordinary share capital is the foundation of any company's financial structure. Business requires that capital be placed at risk and the ultimate bearers of that risk are the ordinary shareholders.

Ordinary shares constitute the ownership capital of a company contributed by the owners and form the most important part of the company's capital. Ordinary shareholders reap the greatest rewards if the company does well and carry the greatest risk if it fails. Ordinary shares have only residual ownership in a company after such priority claims as debentures and preference shares obligations would have been honoured. Ordinary shareholders have a residual claim to any distributable profits left after the other suppliers of capital have been suitably remunerated.

Equities are perpetual capital to the company because the company never pays back the capital acquired through this means. The share capital of a company is usually classified into three authorized, issued and paid-up. The authorized capital is the permissible number of shares that can be issued by a company and fixed in its Memorandum and Articles of Association. The issued capital is the part of the authorized capital that shareholders have

subscribed to while the paid-up capital is the portion of the issued capital that has been paid for by equity holders. Usually issued shares have been paid for. It is uncommon for the issued capital of quoted companies not to be paid for except and occasionally in rights issue.

By law, shares must have a nominal value e.g. they are described as "$1 share" or as "50cent share". This nominal value is usually the price at which the shares were first issued but it may bear no relationship whatsoever to their current market value, It is quite common to find a "$1 share" selling for several Dollars. Occasionally, a company will issue "Stock" rather than "Share". This is purely a difference in packaging. The capital is offered in bulk so that one subscribes for a quantity of it measured in terms of nominal value. stockholder in a company would own, say, $100 of stock while a shareholder would own 100 shares of $1 each. A

Shares issued subsequently to a company's founding fathers may be offered at a price equal to their nominal value (at par) or at a price exceeding their nominal value (at a premium). When shares are issued at a premium, any excess funds raised from the shares are funds raised from the shares above nominal value will be put into a share premium account. Issues may be offered to the general public (a public issue) or restricted to the existing body of shareholders (a rights issue).

Sometimes, a company will issue bonus shares (scrip issues). These are always issued to existing shareholders in proportion to their existing holdings and are free of charge to them. It is important therefore, to note that a bonus issue is not a source of finance as they are not issue for cash. It is a bookkeeping operation performed usually, to give recognition to the fact that legally distributable reserves have become permanently tied up in the business and will not be distributed. In other words, it (bonus issue) is a process of re- capitalization of reserves.

The shares of a quoted company change hands frequently in the Stock Market. This has no direct financial effort on the company, which is not involved in the transactions, except that it is required to maintain an up-to-date register of ownership. The implication of the market to the financial manager is that it constraints the term on which any future issues may be made and thus bears on the cost of capital. The income of the ordinary shareholder is the

residual profit of the company and this he can receive either:
(a) as cash dividend; or

(b)

(c)

as bonus issues as capital appreciation.

Dividends are paid out of the net profit of a company. The decision as to the amount of dividend to be paid, an important one, is determined by the directors of the company and approved by shareholders at the annual general meeting.

In normal circumstances the company is barred by law from repaying capital to its ordinary shareholders. Thus the only way open for withdrawal of capital as investors is by selling their shares on the capital market. In the event of a winding up, the ordinary shareholders are entitled to the proceeds of the

81

whole of the residual assets of the business. This may be a very large amount or it may be nothing at all.

No doubt, the ordinary shareholders are the owners of the company, they are the members of the company and they also, obviously, bear the greatest risk as earlier pointed out Ordinary shareholders have voting rights at general meetings a right not enjoyed by other forms of long-term financing. They determine policies for the company through the board of directors, which they elect. To this end, for a company to attract investors as shareholders, it must promise and deliver high rates of return not only to compensate for the heavy residual risk, but also for inflation risk that might erode future earnings.

A company in need of additional capital may, apart from raising debt instruments, choose to float equity capital for public subscription or tap funds only from its existing shareholders. Capital funding from existing shareholders generally is known as rights issue. In rights offers, new ordinary shares are created to be subscribed to (paid for) by existing shareholders in proportion to their current holdings. Rights issues are an allocation strategy similar to scrips, but unlike scrips, shareholders pay for the additional securities to provide the company with new funds to embark upon desired projects.

In rights, there is no capitalization of reserves as in scrips. To encourage shareholders' participation, rights are often issued at a price usually below the market value. Rights issues are cheaper both to the shareholder and the company. To the shareholder the issue price will be lower than the market price, and the collecting centers will not charge commission for acceptance forms submitted. The issue expenses for the company will be lower than public offers because instead of elaborate prospectus, all the company needs to print is rights circular addressed to each member. A shareholder has the option to exercise or not to exercise his rights. On receipt of rights circular, the shareholder may take any of the following steps:

Take all his rights.

Apply for additional shares in excess of his rights Sell all or part of his rights on the floor of the exchange. Do nothing (iv)

A variant of the equity securities, which is not always resorted to in raising new capital, is the non-voting ordinary shares. As implied in its name, holders of non-voting shares provide funds to a company by way of ordinary shares but do not have a say in the running of the company; a benefit which other equity shareholders have. This method of fund raising might be preferred by companies which are reluctant to further dilute ownership and control.

Beneficiary shares are another variant of ordinary shares. These securities do not form part of a company's share capital, although subscribers are given voting right and also share out of the profit of the company. This class of securities is very uncommon.

Long-term finance may be raised by the issuance of ordinary shares either to new shareholders or to existing shareholders.

If shares are sold to existing shareholders, usually at a price lower than the current market price of

the share, it is called Rights Issue. Thus each shareholder may be entitled to

one share for two shares of stock he already owns. Simply put, the rights issue is 1 for 2. Hence, if a company makes an average annual profit, after tax of N5 million and has two million shares outstanding, at present selling at $70 each. The earnings per share will be:

EPS-

Total carnins No.of Shares $5 million 2 million $2.50

If the company wishes to raise $10 million of new equity funds through a rights offering to shareholders for $50 a share, for each shareholder to buy a share of new stock he will be required to surrender the following number of rights.

(a)

No. of new shares

$50

(b)

No. of rights needed to buy share of the new stock Old Shares 2,000,000

= 10

New Share 200,000

Hence, a shareholder must surrender 10 rights plus $50 to receive one

new share.

The Value of each right

Market Value of Stock - Subcription Price

No. of Rights to buy new share +1

$70 $50 10+ 1

= $1.82

Basically, there are two ways in which ordinary shareholders put funds into their company. It is either by paying for new issues of shares or through

retained profits. Consequently, the market price of the stock will drop by N1.82, i.e. from

$70 to N68.18. Existing shareholders are thus paying $50 for a share worthy N68.18. The rights offering would then devalue the price of the existing stock

by $N1.82.

ADVANTAGES OF ORDINARY SHARE FINANCING 1. During inflation, shares are easier to sell than bonds.

2, Income on ordinary shares is only earned when a company makes profits and the payment of this income is optional. There is no maturity date on ordinary shares. 3.

4. Ordinary shares increase the credit worthiness of a company since it

provides protection to bondholders.

5. Value of share increases with the rising share prices and bonus issues Value of dividend and price of shares move in sympathy with

inflation.

DISADVANTAGES OF ORDINARY SHARE FINANCING

1. Raising funds through ordinary shares dilutes control by increasing the

number of shareholders.

2. The cost of raising finance through ordinary shares offering is usually very high.

3.

Ordinary shares sell at higher yields than other forms of long-term finance. Ordinary share dividends, unlike interest on bonds, are not tax

deductible since they are not expenses.

WHEN TO USE ORDINARY SHARES AS A SOURCE OF FUNDS

1. 2. When leverage is too high When cost of financing is high

3. When inflation is low

4.

5.

When income and profits are unstable

When control is not important.

PREFERENCE SHARE CAPITAL

Preference shares are a form of "hybrid" security between ordinary shares and debentures and are often issued as an alternative to debt when the company pays no tax. In other words preference shares have the features of both debentures and equity. Like equities (ordinary shares), dividend is paid. but like debenture the dividend paid at a fixed rate. Although most preference shares are issued at fixed dividend rate, in the early 1980s preference shares with variable dividend rates developed in the United States. Another debenture feature of preference shares is the non-voting right powers which it carries. Meaning that preference shares do not carry voting rights, hence holders have no right to attend and vote at general meetings.

Again, like ordinary shares, offers for subscription is open to the general public hence a wider capital base. However, preference shares have priority over ordinary shares but are also subordinate to debentures in assets and profits sharing. Suggesting that preference shareholders are given priority over equity holders in the payment of dividend and in the receipt of capital should the company wind-up. Other creditors including bond holders nevertheless take priority over holders of this class of securities in the even of liquidation. The dividend rate on preference share is a percentage of the par value. For example, 10% $1,000 preference share, meaning that a total dividend of $N100 is payable on $1,000 of the stock. In the alternative, 10cent dividend is payable on every $1 of the stock. Dividends on preference shares like equities rank as appropriation of profits and therefore, not regarded as expense of an issuer for tax purposes, hence not tax deductible.

An issuer might opt for preference shares to avoid diluting further the interest of ordinary shareholders in the company. Besides, since dividends are fixed, it enhances budgeting and planning. With respect to the investor, he is assured of specified return and right over ordinary shareholders if the company liquidates. Nonetheless, a disadvantage of this class of shares as against ordinary shares is that holders do not usually (except when it is participating benefit from earnings growth in the company Preference shareholders are neither owners nor creditors of the company.

Moreover, preference shares are either redeemable or irredeemable, cumulative or non-cumulative, convertible or non-convertible as well as participating or non-participating.

CLASSES OF PREFERENCE SHARES

1. REDEEMABLE PREFERENCE SHARES are dated preference shares that the issuing company undertakes to redeem or buy back at a given date.

These are preference shares issued to be rapid at a future date. In some countries, redeemable preference shares are disallowed while of strict conditions required for their issuance in others. InCountry, the Companies and Allied Matters Decree 1990 allows the issuance of redeemable preference shares by a company limited by shares provided it is permitted by its Memorandum and Articles of Association. The redemption or purchase price may be at a premium or at par
830

2. IRREDEEMABLE PREFERENCE SHARES as the name implies, there is no provision for redemption in this case. These classes of shares are also known as undated preference shares, hence no maturity date, The 20 shares remain in a state of performance or perpetuity with the company. Like the ordinary shares, holders can sell them at any time in the Stock Exchange at the current market price to realize their investment.

3. b CUMULATIVE PREFERENCE SHARES are preference shares, which miscarry the right to receive dividend in the current year in addition to dividends, not paid in the previous year(s). In cumulative preference shares, unpaid dividends of previous years must be paid or until cumulative preference shareholders are offered and accepted some alternative compensation for the arrears. Before dividends are paid to ordinary shareholders. No ordinary or other junior dividends are paid before the arrears on cumulative preference shares are made good. All preference shares are cumulative unless expressly designated as non- cumulative. Holder of cumulative preference shares have right to vote at a general meeting only when dividends are in arrears or when it is proposed to change the legal rights of the shares. Generally speaking, cumulative preference shares have a lower dividend rate and more restrict voting right than non-cumulative ones.

NON-CUMULATIVE PREFERENCE SHARES have no right to arrears of dividends. Dividends not paid in one year cannot be carried over to

subsequent years, hence, they are lost for ever. No reference is made to arrears of dividend in subsequent years when the company realize profit. As already mentioned, such dividends is forfeited and lapsed.

PARTICIPATING PREFERENCE SHARES, as the name implies gives the holders limited right to partake in the distributable profit of the company, as well as surplus on liquidation, irrespective of the fixed dividends which accrue to him periodically. In other words, they participate in the amount of profit, if any, remaining when all prior claims have been met. This right to participate in the sharing of profit by way of additional dividends, after receiving the fixed annual dividend rate, will normally be specified in the Articles of Association. For example, a company may restrict preference shareholders to a maximum of 10% of distributable profit in addition to a fixed dividend

rate of 15%.

BOS-PARTICIPATING PREFERENCE SHARES only entitle its holders to a fixed dividend rate often cumulative, but without the right to participate in the sharing of distributable profits after priority claims have been settled.

CONVERTIBLE PREFERENCE SHARES these are preference shares that carry additional right of conversion into equity (ordinary shares) at a specified date and price. Convertible preference shares may be converted, on pre-determined dates and at the option of the holder into ordinary shares of the company at a predetermined rate. Once converted, they cannot be converted back into the original fixed return security (preference shares). When conversion takes place, no money changes hands, holders simply change from one security to another, i.e. from preference shareholder to ordinary shareholder. They provide fixed dividend return for as long as the security remains unconverted and from the point of conversion, they provide the prospect of a capital gain and varying dividend returns. Similarly, on conversion, holder looses all the rights and privileges accruable to preference shareholder while those of ordinary shareholder becomes his.

The conversion right is usually stated as a conversion price or a conversion ratio. A conversion price gives the nominal value of preference share that can be converted into one ordinary share. The conversion ratio gives the number of ordinary shares that will be obtained from the conversion of one unit of preference share. It is generally found that the conversion terms vary over time, with the conversion price increasing in line with the expected increase in ordinary share value. The coupon rate on convertibles is usually lower than non-convertibles because of the expected capital gain. The variability of the conversion terms can be exemplified in the illustration below:

For example, the conversion price of convertible preference share may be that on 1st April 2002, $2 of preference share can be converted into one ordinary share, whereas on 1st April 2003, the conversion price would alter to $2.20 of preference share for one ordinary share.

8. NON-CONVERTIBLE PREFERENCE SHARES are preference shares that maintain their status quo without the option or opportunity to convert into ordinary shares. Holders, at all times, are entitled to all the rights of preference shareholders. In summary, non-convertible preference shares exhibit contrary characteristics as those of convertible preference share in most cases.

Generally, preference shares cannot be secured on the company's asset. The dividend yield, "traditionally" offered on preference dividends has been much too low to provide an attractive investment compared with the interest yields that have been payable on loan stock. From the investors' point of view, these factors make preference shares less attractive, as investment opportunities, than loan stock.

ADVANTAGES OF PREFERENCE SHARES FINANCING 1. Preference shares are non-voting and do not dilute control.

2. Preference shares have no definite maturity date, except they have redeemable feature. 3. Preference shares help to conserve assets, which are then available to be used as collateral for bonds and debentures.

DISADVANTAGES OF PREFERENCE SHARE FINANCING

Preference dividends are not deductible for tax purposes.

Preference shares often sell at higher yields than bonds..

1.

2.

WHEN TO USE PREFERENCE SHARES FOR RAISING FUNDS

When leverage is required, yet profit are not very high.

1.

2. When costs of preference shares are low in relation to those of ordinary shares. When leverage is already high in relation to industrial average and

3.

control is important.

DEBENTURES, LOAN STOCKS AND LOAN

Debentures, loan stocks and loans are debt instruments of interest- bearing securities, bearing specified interest payments and maturity dates. On maturity, the principal is redeemed (liquidated). Redemption can either be affected on a specified day (e.g. 30th June 2010) or stretched over a period of time (e.g. by annual instalment starting from 30th June 2006 to 30th June 2010 in which case five annual instalments will be made). Whatever mode of

87

redemption is adopted, proper disclosure must be made in the offer document Debt instruments are evidence by certificates, which disclose important features of the instruments.

DEBENTURES are a form of loan stock, legally defined as the written

acknowledgement of a debt incurred by a company. usually given under the company seal and normally containing provisions about the payment of interes

and the eventual repayment of capital. Besides, debentures are long-term

promissory notes issued by a borrowing company to the lender acknowledging a

substantial debt on which interest is earned. They are also called BONDS

Holders of debentures are known as debenture holders.

LOAN STOCK, on the other hand, is a long-term debt capital raised by a company for which interest is paid, usually half yearly and at a fixed rate Holders of loan stock are therefore long-term CI CDITORS of the company Loan stock has nominal value, which is the debt owed by the company, and interest is paid at a stated "coupon yield" on this amount. For example, if a company issues 10% loan stock, the coupon yield will be 10% of the nominal value of the stock, so that $100 of stock will receive

$10 interest each year.

LOANS, particularly bank loans, are popularly becoming form of long- term funds for companies in that they are generally easier to obtain, and can often be cheaper, since interest payment are tax deductible, However, they usually attract and necessitate some form of security being given, Loans are repayment debts at stated date. In case of default, the collateral provided are disposed off and the proceeds used to redeem the loan.

The coupon (interest) rates carried by these instruments can either be fixed or floating. Fixed rate securities pay fixed interest rate, clearly specified at the time of issue. Such rates are not variable but remain static throughout the life span of the instrument. The coupon rates are usually expressed as percentage of the par value when issued, albeit secondary trading could be at a premium or discount depending on investors' perception of the issue and prevailing economic circumstances. Fixed rate securities are more commonly used in times of relative stability in interest rates. However, in periods of high rate volatility, floating rates could be adjusted upwards or downwards in line with general trends in market rates Floating rates instruments can therefore be defined as debt securities attracting variable coupon rates. The rates are reviewed and adjusted periodically using the Minimum Rediscount Rate (MRR) or other money market rates such as treasury bill rates as reference for adjustment. MRR serves as the reference rate for floating securities. An illustration: the coupon rate at the time of a security issue could be 17%, that is 2% above a current MRR of say 15% subject to a maximum of 25% above and a minimum of 14%. This in essence means that the maximum rate at any given time would not exceed 25% while the minimum rate would not fall below 14%. The applicable coupon rate would consequently float between 14% and 29%

88
Both fixed and floating rate securities have their advantages and disadvantages to both the issuer and the investor Since applicable coupon rates are known as initial in fixed rate securities, the issuer can compute in advance the total cost of servicing the debt. This would enable smooth planning. On the other hand, planning is much more difficult in floating rate securities, as projections regarding the total cost of debt servicing cannot be accurately determined. A disadvantage of the fixed rate security is that, being static, interest rate

cannot be varied even when market rates drop sharply after the security has

been issued. The issuers would thus, be burdened with high interest payments

However, any rise in market rates after floatation would be advantageous to the

issuer as he would be saved the additional funds for higher interest obligation The variability of floating rates may be beneficial to issuers if rates fall below the reference point, but it is not unusual to have a benchmark stipulated to guarantee a minimum return on the invested sums. The fixed rate investor gains when prevailing market rates fall below the interest on his fixed security. His gain is the difference between the market rate and the fixed rate. He would make a loss if the converse happens. The advantage of the floating rate has earlier been stated. Regular adjustment of rares en es the holder of such instruments to hedge against capital losses, which might arise from interest rate instability

Prior to the introduction of the Structural Adjustment Programme (SAP) in 1986, interest rates were administratively, determined and deliberately kept low to encourage investment, and the growth of certain preferred sectors in the economy. This created distortions in the allocation of resources and encouraged the use of short-term funds for long-term finance; an obvious mismatch and hindrance to capital market growth. During this period. long-term debt securities also carried fixed coupon rates. Being officially determined, money market rates were relatively stable, Thus, the use of fixed coupon rates on long term debt securities seemed appropriate. Following the liberalization of money market rates, floating rates were introduced in the capital market and have since become popular Applying floating rates to debt securities following SAP has therefore become necessary to enhance the competitiveness of corporate debt instruments to investors vis-à-vis money

market rates. The life span of long term debt instruments usually stretches from five years to perpetuity. However, perpetual issues and issues of less than five years are quite uncommon. In Nigeria, most issues are between 5 to 15 years. When an issue is perpetual no fixed rate of maturity would be attached to it, it might indeed be held forever and usually captioned "Irredeemable Debenture (or Loan) "Stock". Because of its features, it is relatively illiquid although the coupon rates are usually more attractive than non-perpetual bonds.

7100 Some interest bearing securities carry "CALL FEATURES" which allows the issuer to redeem the security at a specified call price before the maturity date. A bond having a maturity of 20 years could carry a call feature giving the issuer the night to recall the issue after 10 years. The call price is usually higher than the redemption price had the security matured. For instance, if a

89

security is to be redeemed at a par value of $100 the call price could be $116 thus, offering a call premium of $10. The reason for the premium is to compensate the holder for early redemption of the issue. The call option often exercised by issuers when market rate of interest drops below fixed rate instruments of the issuers. This saves the issuer high interest payments had he not "called" the security. Example, if the coupon rate of a fixed rate issue i 15% and market rate of interest falls to 12%, it might be advisable for the issue to exercise his right to call the issue. This saves the issuer the burden of paying a rate higher than the market rate of interest thus resulting in avoided obligation of 3% on his issue. Nonetheless, issuers should consider other factors as well, in deciding on whether or not to exercise the option to call in the security. To the investor, the early redemption of the issue could enable him place his funds in more profitable instruments that may be available to him.

and The terms of redemption would be contained in a trust deed (indenture every corporate debt issuer is required by law in most jurisdictions to appoint a qualified trustee under whose authority the property and money relating to the debt issue would be vested. The trustee in his relationship to the issuer must be free from any form of conflict of interest if he is to perform his duties in the best interest of the stockholders whom he represents. Generally, the trust deed would contain other relevant information pertaining to the issue such as the amount being raised, the par value, coupon rate, type of issue (e.g secured, unsecured, floating or fixed rate), protective covenants, call provision if any and property under pledge. Such information would be released at the primary market stage through disclosures in the prospectus. A protective covenant is intended to protect the stockholders as it spells out the "dos and don'ts" of the issuer. For instance it could restrict the borrowing power of the issuer and touch on such issues as working capital, debt-equity ratio etc. Besides, a trust deed would empower a trustee (such as an insurance company or a bank) to intervene on behalf of debenture holders if the conditions of borrowing under which the debentures were issued are not being fulfilled. This might involves:

(a) Failure to pay interest on the due dates. (b) An attempt by the company to sell off important assets contrary to the terms of the loans.

(c) A situation where a company takes out other additional loans and thereby exceeds previously agreed borrowing limits established either by the Articles or by the specific terms of the debenture trust deed. A trust deed might well place restrictions on the company's ability to borrow more from elsewhere until the debentures have been redeemed.

CLASSES OF DEBENTURES

Legally, the holder of debenture or loan stock is a creditor of the company who has a right to a fixed annual return with the promise d repayment of a fixed money sum either after a set term or on the winding up d the company. Classes of debenture include:

UNSECURED DEBENTURE (LOAN STOCK)

Not all loans are secured. Unsecured debentures are also known as NAKED debentures. The holders have no special rights; they have the same right as ordinary creditors. In the event of liquidation, they are repaid after secured debenture holders, but before preference and ordinary shareholders. A lender of unsecured loan stock cannot however limit the amount of fixed and floating charges given as security to other lenders, except in so far as the total borrowing capability of the company may be restricted by the unsecured loan agreement.

Investors are likely to expect a higher yield with unsecured loan stock to compensate them for the extra risk involved in holding them. The rate of interest on unsecured loan stock may be around 1% higher than for secured debentures. Unsecured debenture means that no pledge has been made by the company against its assets. In other words, in the event of the company winding up investors would have no claim on its assets. Debentures are issued against the performance record of the company.

2. SECURED DEBENTURE

In secured debenture stock, the company (issuer) pledges specific assets disclose in the trust deed, which in the case of default, stockholders would have a claim on. A secured debenture may be pledged against specific asset of the company (fixed charge) or on all its assets (floating charge). For the recovery of principal in the event of liquidation, the secured debt holder has priority over his unsecured counterpart and indeed over all creditors. A debenture stock can carry a "NEGATIVE PLEDGE clause which would

forbid the issuer (company) from issuing any debt instrument to new stockholders seeking to confer rights in respect of claims on assets superior to

those of the existing stockholders.

DEBENTURE SECURED BY FLOATING CHARGE means that the charge FLOATS over the assets of the company, excluding those mortgaged, during which the company has complete power of sale or purchase of assets. If the company defaults, the charge is brought down on the assets of the company. The lender can choose which assets to crystallize as security in the event of a default of payment provided that another lender does not have a prior charge on the asset.

DEBENTURE SECURED BY FIXED CHARGE connotes that the charge is on one or more specific assets, usually land and building plant and machinery, motor vehicles, which are mortgaged thus depriving the company of the documents of the title. The company would be unable to dispose of the asset without providing a substitute asset for security or without the lender's consent. In the event of liquidation, the asset will be sold and the proceeds applied first in reduction of the debt to those mortgage debenture holders.

The best security is a fixed charge on a specific asset plas a floating charge on say, the current assets of the company. Such security however,
would imply high risk and uncertainty about the borrower Lenders will be careful to ensure that they have adequate security, therefore there will be limit to the amount of secured borrowing that a company can make without acquiring more assets to offer as security.

Debenture holders secured on floating charge and the unsecured loun stock, are in a somewhat similar position to that of the shareholders, an that the security of their investment is heavily dependent upon the success value of a particular asset. They do however have the additional security of ranking before shareholders in the event of a liquidation.

3 REDEEMABLE DEBENTURE

Redeemable denture has promise of repayment of capital sum at a predetermined future time. In other words, the redemption date is usually fixed, and the borrower is not allowed to redeem it at will, except "call feature is provided for. Redeemable debentures are also called dated debentures However, in certain cases redemption is allowed and more preferably when.

(i) The borrower wishes to dispose of an asset upon which a debenture is

secured. The borrower has surplus funds, which cannot be invested profitably The borrower wishes to alter its capital structure.

If the debentures to be issued are redeemable, the company must be very careful in determining the optimum timing for the refunding. The main factor will be to minimize the present value of all costs associated with the decision. These costs include costs of refinancing the debts, costs of the redemption process and opportunity costs of investment opportunities foregone due to early debt redemption.

(a)

METHODS OF RAISING FUNDS FOR REDEMPTION

There is Creating new debts to finance old ones. In other words, a company will repay old debt by raising cash from a new loan, thus renewing its borrowing, albeit, perhos at a different.: interest rate. guarantee that a company will be able to become a new loan to pay off maturing debt, and one item to look for in a company's balance sheet is to the redemption date of current loans, to establish how much new finance

b) is likely to be needed by the company and when. Creating sinking fund where specific amount would be paid annually over the life span of e debt to equate the debt eventually. A sinking fund is a special account into which regular equal payment is made to Jo meet interest obligations as they fall due, and more importantly liquidate the debt at maturity

Redemption through reserves and retained earnings. Creating new shareholders or expanding the base of the exist shareholders by issuance of new shares to be subscribed to. Disposal of assets-last resor...

92
4.

IRREDEEMABLE DENTURES

These are debt capital with no fixed date of redemption. Package in another fashion, they are also referred to as undated debentures. Borrowers enjoy the use forever, so long as the company is having an encouraging "going

concern status". Payment of agreed interest rate is maintained by the borrower.

5.

NON-CONVERTIBLE DEBENTURES A debenture stock is tagged non-convertible when the stock does not

give the holder the option to exchange his debt instrument for ordinary shares at a later date. Non-convertible debenture has no warrants issue along with it, hence the stockholder remains a debenture holder as long as the company lives, and again depending on whether the debenture is redeemable or irredeemable.

6.

CONVERTIBLE DEBENTURES

A convertible debenture stock is one which is gives the holders the option

to exchange his debt instrument for ordinary shares at a later date. To enhance the marketability of a debt security or preference shares at issue, a company may decide to issue warrants along with the debenture stock. The warrant would give the stockholder the right to purchase proportionate amount of the company's shares at a predetermined price for perpetuity or for a given period of years after which it expires. When the stockholder wishes to exercise his right, new shares would be created by the company. The exercise price of warrants is often higher than the market price of the issuing company's equities at the time the warrant was issued.

Convertible debentures are ordinary redeemable debenture and loan stock except that holders have the option to convert them into a certain number of ordinary shares at a fixed time or period in the future. When conversion takes place no money changes hands, holders simply change from one security to another. Once converted they cannot be converted back into the original fixed return security. The conversion right is usually stated as a conversion price or a conversion ratio. The conversion price gives the nominal value of loan stock that can be converted into one ordinary share.

The conversion ratio gives the number of ordinary shares that will be obtained from the conversion of one unit of loan stock. It is generally found that the conversion terms vary over time, with the conversion price increasing in line with the expected increase in ordinary share value. Convertible debentures have the characteristics of both equity and debt.

They provide a fixed interest return for as long as the security remain unconverted, and also provide the prospect of a capital gain through converting into more valuable ordinary shares. The coupon rate on convertibles is usually lower than on ordinary debentures because of the expected capital gain.

Convertible often do not carry any security in which case they are called convertible unsecured loan stock.

www.ingramcontent.com/pod-product-compliance
Lightning Source LLC
Chambersburg PA
CBHW062325290526
45794CB00005B/1897